On the Catechising of the Uninstructed

On the Catechising of the Uninstructed

St. Augustine

On the Catechising of the Uninstructed

© Lighthouse Publishing 2018

Translated by Rev. S.D.F Salmond, D.D

Updated into Modern U.S English by A.M. Overett

All rights reserved. Without limiting the rights under copyright reserved above, no part of this publication may be reproduced, stored in a retrieval system, or transmitted, in any form or by any means (electronic, mechanical, photocopying, recording or otherwise), without the prior written permission of the copyright owner of this book.

Published by
Lighthouse Christian Publishing
SAN 257-4330
5531 Dufferin Drive
Savage, Minnesota, 55378
United States of America

www.lighthousechristianpublishing.com

Introductory Notice.

In the fourteenth chapter of the second book of his Retractations, Augustin makes the following statement: "There is also a book of ours on the subject of the Catechising of the Uninstructed, [or, for Instructing the Unlearned, De Catechizandis Rudibus], that being, indeed, the express title by which it is designated. In this book, where I have said, 'Neither did the angel, who, in company with other spirits who were his satellites, forsook in pride the obedience of God, and became the devil, do any hurt to God, but to himself; for God knoweth how to dispose of souls that leave Him:' it would be more appropriate to say, 'spirits that leave Him,' inasmuch as the question dealt with angels. This book commences in these terms: 'You have requested me, brother Deogratias.'"

The composition so described in the passage cited is reviewed by Augustin regarding other works which he had in hand about the year 400 A.D., and may therefore be taken to belong to that date. It has been conjectured that the person to whom it is addressed may perhaps be the same with the presbyter Deogratias, to whom, as we read in the epistle which now ranks as the hundred and second, Augustin wrote about the year 406, in reply to some questions of the pagans which were forwarded to him from Carthage.

The Benedictine editors introduce the treatise in the following terms: "At the request of a deacon of Carthage, Augustin undertakes the task of teaching the art of catechising; and in the first place, he gives certain injunctions, to the effect that this kind of duty may be discharged not only in a settled method and an apt order, but also without tediousness, and in a spirit of cheerfulness. Thereafter reducing his injunctions to practical use, he gives an example of what he means by delivering two set discourses, presenting parallels to each other, the one being somewhat lengthened and the other very brief, but both suitable for the instruction of any individual whose desire is to be a Christian."

[This treatise shows what was thought in the age of Saint Augustin to be the most needful instruction in religion. The Latin text: De Cactechizandis Rudibus, is in the sixth vol. of the Benedictine edition, and in the handy ed. of C. Marriott: S. Augustini Opuscula quædam, Oxford and London (Parker & Co.) 4th ed. 1885. An earlier and closer English Version by Rev. C. L. Cornish, M. A., of Exeter College, Oxford, appeared in the Oxford "Library of the Fathers" (1847, pp. 187 sqq.,) under the title On Instructing the Unlearned. H. De Romestin reproduces the Oxford translation in the English version of Marriott's ed. of five treatises of St. Augustin, Oxford and London, 1885, pp. 1–71.—P.S.]

Chapter 1. —How Augustin Writes in Answer to a Favor Asked by a Deacon of Carthage.

1. You have requested me, brother Deogratias, to send you in writing something which might be of service to you in the matter of catechising the uninstructed. For you have informed me that in Carthage, where you hold the position of a deacon, persons, who have to be taught the Christian faith from its very rudiments, are frequently brought to you by reason of your enjoying the reputation of possessing a rich gift in catechising, due at once to an intimate acquaintance with the faith, and to an attractive method of discourse; but that you almost always find yourself in a difficulty as to the manner in which a suitable declaration is to be made of the precise doctrine, the belief of which constitutes us Christians: regarding the point at which our statement of the same ought to commence, and the limit to which it should be allowed to proceed: and with respect to the question whether, when our narration is concluded, we ought to make use of any kind of exhortation, or simply specify those precepts in the observance of which the person to whom we are discoursing may know the Christian life and profession to be maintained. At the same time, you have made the confession and complaint that it has often befallen you that in the course of a lengthened and languid address you have become profitless and distasteful even to yourself, not to speak of the learner whom you have been endeavoring to instruct by your utterance, and the other parties who have been present as hearers; and that you have been constrained by these straits to put upon me the constraint of that love which I owe to you, so that I may not feel it a burdensome thing among all my engagements to write you something on this subject.

2. As for myself then, if, in the exercise of those capacities which through the bounty of our Lord I am enabled to present, the same Lord requires me to offer any

manner of aid to those whom He has made brethren to me, I feel constrained not only by that love and service which is due from me to you on the terms of familiar friendship, but also by that which I owe universally to my mother the Church, by no means to refuse the task, but rather to take it up with a prompt and devoted willingness. For the more extensively I desire to see the treasure of the Lord distributed, the more does it become my duty, if I ascertain that the stewards, who are my fellow-servants, find any difficulty in laying it out, to do all that lies in my power to the end that they may be able to accomplish easily and expeditiously what they sedulously and earnestly aim at.

Chapter 2. —How It Often Happens that a Discourse Which Gives Pleasure to the Hearer is Distasteful to the Speaker; And What Explanation is to Be Offered of that Fact.

3. But as regards the idea thus privately entertained by yourself in such efforts, I would not have you to be disturbed by the consideration that you have often appeared to yourself to be delivering a poor and wearisome discourse. For it may very well be the case that the matter has not so presented itself to the person whom you were trying to instruct, but that what you were uttering seemed to you to be unworthy of the ears of others, simply because it was your own earnest desire that there should be something better to listen to. Indeed with me, too, it is almost always the fact that my speech displeases myself. For I am covetous of something better, the possession of which I frequently enjoy within me before I commence to body it forth in intelligible words: and then when my capacities of expression prove inferior to my inner apprehensions, I grieve over the inability which my tongue has betrayed in answering to my heart. For it is my wish that he who hears me should have the same complete understanding of the subject which I have myself; and I perceive that I fail to speak in a manner calculated to effect that, and that this arises mainly from the circumstance that the intellectual

apprehension diffuses itself through the mind with something like a rapid flash, whereas the utterance is slow, and occupies time, and is of a vastly different nature, so that, while this latter is moving on, the intellectual apprehension has already withdrawn itself within its secret abodes. Yet, in consequence of its having stamped certain impressions of itself in a marvelous manner upon the memory, these prints endure with the brief pauses of the syllables; and as the outcome of these same impressions we form intelligible signs, which get the name of a certain language, either the Latin, or the Greek, or the Hebrew, or some other. And these signs may be objects of thought, or they may also be actually uttered by the voice. On the other hand however, the impressions themselves are neither Latin, nor Greek, nor Hebrew, nor peculiar to any other race whatsoever, but are made good in the mind just as looks are in the body. For anger is designated by one word in Latin, by another in Greek, and by different terms in other languages, according to their several diversities. But the look of the angry man is neither (peculiarly) Latin nor (peculiarly) Greek. Thus it is that when a person says Iratus sum, he is not understood by every nation, but only by the Latins; whereas, if the mood of his mind when it is kindling to wrath comes forth upon the face and affects the look, all who have the individual within their view under the intellectual apprehension stamps upon the memory, and to hold them forth, as it were, to the perception of the hearers by means of the sound of the voice, in any manner parallel to the clear and evident form in which the look appears. For those former are within in the mind, while this latter is without in the body. Wherefore we have to surmise how far the sound of our mouth must be from representing that stroke of the intelligence, seeing that it does not correspond even with the impression produced upon the memory. Now, it is a common occurrence with us that, in the ardent desire to effect what is of profit to our hearer, our aim is to express ourselves to him exactly as our intellectual apprehension is at the time, when, in the very effort, we are failing in the ability to speak; and then, because this does not succeed with us, we are vexed, and we pine in weariness as if we were applying ourselves to vain labors; and, as the result of this very weariness, our discourse becomes itself more languid and pointless even than it was when it first induced such a sense of tediousness.

4. But ofttimes the earnestness of those who are desirous of hearing me shows me that my utterance is not so frigid as it seems to myself to be. From the delight, too, which they exhibit, I gather that they derive some profit from it. And I occupy myself sedulously with the endeavor not to fail in putting before them a service in which I perceive them to take in such good part what is put before them. Even, so, on your side also, the very fact that persons who require to be instructed in the faith are brought so frequently to you, ought to help you to understand that your discourse is not displeasing to others as it is displeasing to yourself; and you ought not to consider yourself unfruitful, simply because you do not succeed in setting forth in such a manner as you desire the things which you discern; for, perchance, you may be just as little able to discern them in the way you wish. For in this life who sees except as "in an enigma and through a glass"? Neither is love itself of might sufficient to rend the darkness of the flesh, and penetrate into that eternal calm from which even things which pass away derive the light in which they shine. But inasmuch as day by day the good are making advances towards the vision of that day, independent of the rolling sky, and without the invasion of the night, "which eye hath not seen, nor ear heard, neither hath it entered into the heart of man," there is no greater reason why our discourse should become valueless in our own estimate, when we are engaged in teaching the uninstructed, than this,—namely, that it is a delight to us to discern in an extraordinary fashion, and a weariness to speak in an ordinary. And in reality, we are listened to with much greater satisfaction, indeed, when we ourselves also have pleasure in the same work; for the thread of our address is affected by the very joy of which we ourselves are sensible, and it proceeds from us with greater ease and with more acceptance. Consequently, as regards those matters which are recommended as articles of belief,

the task is not a difficult one to lay down injunctions, with respect to the points at which the narration should be commenced and ended, or with respect to the method in which the narration is to be varied, so that at one time it may be briefer, at another more lengthened, and yet at all times full and perfect; and, again, with respect to the particular occasions on which it may be right to use the shorter form, and those on which it will be proper to employ the longer. But as to the means by which all is to be done, so that everyone may have pleasure in his work when he catechises (for the better he succeeds in this the more attractive will he be), —that is what requires the greatest consideration. And yet we have not far to seek for the precept which will rule in this sphere. For if, in the matter of carnal means, God loves a cheerful giver, how much more so in that of the spiritual? But our security that this cheerfulness may be with us at the seasonable hour, is something dependent upon the mercy of Him who has given us such precepts. Therefore, in accordance with my understanding of what your own wish is, we shall discuss in the first place the subject of the method of narration, then that of the duty of delivering injunction and exhortation, and afterwards that of the attainment of the said cheerfulness, so far as God may furnish us with the ideas.

Chapter 3. —Of the Full Narration to Be Employed in Catechising.

5. The narration is full when each person is catechised in the first instance from what is written in the text, "In the beginning God created the heaven and the earth," on to the present times of the Church. This does not imply, however, either that we ought to repeat by memory the entire Pentateuch, and the entire Books of Judges, and Kings, and Esdras, and the entire Gospel and Acts of the Apostles, if we have learned all these word for word; or that we should put all the matters which are contained in these volumes into our own words, and in that manner unfold and expound them as a whole. For neither does the time admit

of that, nor does any necessity demand it. But what we ought to do is, to give a comprehensive statement of all things, summarily and generally, so that certain of the more wonderful facts may be selected which are listened to with superior gratification, and which have been ranked so remarkably among the exact turning-points (of the history); that, instead of exhibiting them to view only in their wrappings, if we may so speak, and then instantly snatching them from our sight, we ought to dwell on them for a certain space, and thus, as it were, unfold them and open them out to vision, and present them to the minds of the hearers as things to be examined and admired. But as for all other details, these should be passed over rapidly, and thus far introduced and woven into the narrative. The effect of pursuing this plan is, that the particular facts which we wish to see specially commended to attention obtain greater prominence in consequence of the others being made to yield to them; while, at the same time, neither does the learner, whose interest we are anxious to stimulate by our statement, come to these subjects with a mind already exhausted, nor is confusion induced upon the memory of the person whom we ought to be instructing by our teaching.

6. In all things, indeed, not only ought our own eye to be kept fixed upon the end of the commandment, which is "charity, out of a pure heart, and a good conscience, and faith unfeigned," to which we should make all that we utter refer; but in like manner ought the gaze of the person whom we are instructing by our utterance to be moved toward the same, and guided in that direction. And, in truth, for no other reason were all those things which we read in the Holy Scriptures written, previous to the Lord's advent, but for this,—namely, that His advent might be pressed upon the attention, and that the Church which was to be, should be intimated beforehand, that is to say, the people of God throughout all nations; which Church is His body, wherewith also are united and numbered all the saints who lived in this world, even before His advent, and who believed then in His future coming, just as we believe in His past coming. For (to use an illustration) Jacob, at the time

when he was being born, first put forth from the womb a hand, with which also he held the foot of the brother who was taking priority of him in the act of birth; and next indeed the head followed, and thereafter, at last, and as matter of course, the rest of the members: while, nevertheless the head in point of dignity and power has precedence, not only of those members which followed it then, but also of the very hand which anticipated it in the process of the birth, and is really the first, although not in the matter of the time of appearing, at least in the order of nature. And in an analogous manner, the Lord Jesus Christ, previous to His appearing in the flesh, and coming forth in a certain manner out of the womb of His secrecy, before the eyes of men as Man, the Mediator between God and men, "who is over all, God blessed forever," sent before Him, in the person of the holy patriarchs and prophets, a certain portion of His body, wherewith, as by a hand, He gave token before time of His own approaching birth, and also supplanted the people who were prior to Him in their pride, using for that purpose the bonds of the law, as if they were His five fingers. For through five epochs of times there was no cessation in the foretelling and prophesying of His own destined coming; and in a manner consonant with this, he through whom the law was given wrote five books; and proud men, who were carnally minded, and sought to "establish their own righteousness," were not filled with blessing by the open hand of Christ, but were debarred from such good by the hand compressed and closed; and therefore their feet were tied, and "they fell, while we are risen, and stand upright." But although, as I have said, the Lord Christ did thus send before Him a certain portion of His body, in the person of those holy men who came before Him as regards the time of birth, nevertheless He is Himself the Head of the body, the Church, and all these have been attached to that same body of which He is the head, in virtue of their believing in Him whom they announced prophetically. For they were not sundered (from that body) in consequence of fulfilling their course before Him, but rather were they made one with the same by reason of their obedience. For although the hand may be put forward away before the head, still it has its connection beneath the head. Wherefore all things which were written aforetime were written in order that we might be taught thereby, and were our figures, and happened in a figure in the case of these men. Moreover they were written for our sakes, upon whom the end of the ages has come.

Chapter 4. —That the Great Reason for the Advent of Christ Was the Commendation of Love.

7. Moreover, what greater reason is apparent for the advent of the Lord than that God might show His love in us, commending it powerfully, inasmuch as "while we were yet sinners, Christ died for us"? And furthermore, this is with the intent that, inasmuch as charity is "the end of the commandment," and "the fulfilling of the law," we also may love one another and lay down our life for the brethren, even as He laid down His life for us. And with regard to God Himself, its object is that, even if it were an irksome task to love Him, it may now at least cease to be irksome for us to return His love, seeing that "He first loved us," and "spared not His own only Son, but delivered Him up for us all." For there is no mightier invitation to love than to anticipate in loving; and that soul is over hard which, supposing it unwilling indeed to give love, is unwilling also to give the return of love. But if, even in the case of criminal and sordid loves, we see how those who desire to be loved in return make it their special and absorbing business, by such proofs as are within their power, to render the strength of the love which they themselves bear plain and patent; if we also perceive how they affect to put forward an appearance of justice in what they thus offer, such as may qualify them in some sort to demand that a response be made in all fairness to them on the part of those souls which they are laboring to beguile; if, further, their own passion burns more vehemently when they observe that the minds which they are eager to possess are also moved now by the same fire: if thus, I say, it happens at once that the soul which before was

torpid is excited so soon as it feels itself to be loved, and that the soul which was enkindled already becomes the more inflamed so soon as it is made cognizant of the return of its own love, it is evident that no greater reason is to be found why love should be either originated or enlarged, than what appears in the occasion when one who as yet loves not at all comes to know himself to be the object of love, or when one who is already a lover either hopes that he may yet be loved in turn, or has by this time the evidence of a response to his affection. And if this holds good even in the case of base loves, how much more in (true) friendship? For what else have we carefully to attend to in this question touching the injuring of friendship than to this, namely, not to give our friend cause to suppose either that we do not love him at all, or that we love him less than he loves us? If, indeed, he is led to entertain this belief, he will be cooler in that love in which men enjoy the interchange of intimacies one with another; and if he is not of that weak type of character to which such an offense to affection will serve as a cause of freezing off from love altogether, he yet confines himself to that kind of affection in which he loves, not with the view of enjoyment to himself, but with the idea of studying the good of others. But again, it is worth our while to notice how, —although superiors also have the wish to be loved by their inferiors, and are gratified with the zealous attention paid to them by such, and themselves cherish greater affection towards these inferiors the more they become cognizant of that, —with what might of love, nevertheless, the inferior kindles so soon as he learns that he is beloved by his superior. For there have we love in its more grateful aspect, where it does not consume itself in the drought of want, but flows forth in the plenteousness of beneficence. For the former type of love is of misery, the latter of mercy. And furthermore, if the inferior was despairing even of the possibility of his being loved by his superior, he will now be inexpressibly moved to love if the superior has of his own will condescended to show how much he loves this person who could by no means be bold enough to promise himself so great a good. But what is there superior to God in the character of Judge? and what more desperate than man in the character of sinner? —than man, I ask, who had given himself all the more unreservedly up to the wardship and domination of proud powers which are unable to make him blessed, as he had come more absolutely to despair of the possibility of his being an object of interest to that power which wills not to be exalted in wickedness, but is exalted in goodness.

8. If, therefore, it was mainly for this purpose that Christ came, to wit, that man might learn how much God loves him; and that he might learn this, to the intent that he might be kindled to the love of Him by whom he was first loved, and might also love his neighbor at the command and showing of Him who became our neighbor, in that He loved man when, instead of being a neighbor to Him, he was sojourning far apart: if, again, all divine Scripture, which was written aforetime, was written with the view of presignifying the Lord's advent; and if whatever has been committed to writing in times subsequent to these, and established by divine authority, is a record of Christ, and admonishes us of love, it is manifest that on those two commandments of love to God and love to our neighbor hang not only all the law and the prophets, which at the time when the Lord spoke to that effect were as yet the only Holy Scripture, but also all those books of the divine literature which have been written at a later period for our health, and consigned to remembrance. Wherefore, in the Old Testament there is a veiling of the New, and in the New Testament there is a revealing of the Old. According to that veiling, carnal men, understanding things in a carnal fashion, have been under the dominion, both then and now, of a penal fear. According to this revealing, on the other hand, spiritual men, —among whom we reckon at once those then who knocked in piety and found even hidden things opened to them, and others now who seek in no spirit of pride, lest even things uncovered should be closed to them, —understanding in a spiritual fashion, have been made free through the love wherewith they have been gifted. Consequently, inasmuch as there is nothing more adverse to love than envy, and as pride is the mother of envy, the same

Lord Jesus Christ, God-man, is both a manifestation of divine love towards us, and an example of human humility with us, to the end that our great swelling might be cured by a greater counteracting remedy. For here is great misery, proud man! But there is greater mercy, a humble God! Take this love, therefore, as the end that is set before you, to which you are to refer all that you say, and, whatever you narrate, narrate it in such a manner that he to whom you are discoursing on hearing may believe, on believing may hope, on hoping may love.

Chapter 5. —That the Person Who Comes for Catechetical Instruction is to Be Examined with Respect to His Views, on Desiring to Become a Christian.

9. Moreover, it is on the ground of that very severity of God, by which the hearts of mortals are agitated with a most wholesome terror, that love is to be built up; so that, rejoicing that he is loved by Him whom he fears, man may have boldness to love Him in return, and yet at the same time be afraid to displease His love toward himself, even should he be able to do so with impunity. For certainly it very rarely happens, nay, I should rather say, never, that anyone approaches us with the wish to become a Christian who has not been smitten with some sort of fear of God. For if it is in the expectation of some advantage from men whom he deems himself unlikely to please in any other way, or with the idea of escaping any disadvantage at the hands of men of whose displeasure or hostility he is seriously afraid, that a man wishes to become a Christian, then his wish to become one is not so earnest as his desire to feign one. For faith is not a matter of the body which does obeisance, but of the mind which believes. But unmistakably it is often the case that the mercy of God comes to be present through the ministry of the catechiser, so that, affected by the discourse, the man now wishes to become in reality that which he had made up his mind only to feign. And so soon as he begins to have this manner of desire, we may judge him then to have made a genuine approach to us. It is true, indeed, that the

precise time when a man, whom we perceive to be present with us already in the body, comes to us in reality with his mind, is a thing hidden from us. But, notwithstanding that, we ought to deal with him in such a manner that this wish may be made to arise within him, even should it not be there at present. For no such labor is lost, inasmuch as, if there is any wish at all, it is assuredly strengthened by such action on our part, although we may be ignorant of the time or the hour at which it began. It is useful certainly, if it can be done, to get from those who know the man some idea beforehand of the state of mind in which he is, or of the causes which have induced him to come with the view of embracing religion. But if there is no other person available from whom we may gather such information, then, indeed, the man himself is to be interrogated, so that from what he says in reply we may draw the beginning of our discourse. Now if he has come with a false heart, desirous only of human advantages or thinking to escape disadvantages, he will certainly speak what is untrue. Nevertheless, the very untruth which he utters should be made the point from which we start. This should not be done, however, with the (open) intention of confuting his falsehood, as if that were a settled matter with you; but, taking it for granted that he has professed to have come with a purpose which is really worthy of approbation (whether that profession be true or false), it should rather be our aim to commend and praise such a purpose as that with which, in his reply, he has declared himself to have come; so that we may make him feel it a pleasure to be the kind of man actually that he wishes to seem to be. On the other hand, supposing him to have given a declaration of his views other than what ought to be before the mind of one who is to be instructed in the Christian faith, then by reproving him with more than usual kindness and gentleness, as a person uninstructed and ignorant, by pointing out and commending, concisely and in a grave spirit the end of Christian doctrine in its genuine reality, and by doing all this in such a manner as neither to anticipate the times of a narration, which should be given subsequently, nor to venture to impose that kind of statement upon a mind not previously set for it, you may bring him to desire that which, either in mistake or in dissimulation, he has not been desiring up to this stage.

Chapter 6. —Of the Way to Commence the Catechetical Instruction, and of the Narration of Facts from the History of the World's Creation on to the Present Times of the Church.

10. But if it happens that his answer is to the effect that he has met with some divine warning, or with some divine terror, prompting him to become a Christian, this opens up the way most satisfactorily for a commencement to our discourse, by suggesting the greatness of God's interest in us. His thoughts, however, ought certainly to be turned away from this line of things, whether miracles or dreams, and directed to the more solid path and the surer oracles of the Scriptures; so that he may also come to understand how mercifully that warning was administered to him in advance, previous to his giving himself to the Holy Scriptures. And assuredly it ought to be pointed out to him, that the Lord Himself would neither thus have admonished him and urged him on to become a Christian, and to be incorporated into the Church, nor have taught him by such signs or revelations, had it not been His will that, for his greater safety and security, he should enter upon a pathway already prepared in the Holy Scriptures, in which he should not seek after visible miracles, but learn the habit of hoping for things invisible, and in which also he should receive monitions not in sleep but in wakefulness. At this point the narration ought now to be commenced, which should start with the fact that God made all things very good, and which should be continued, as we have said, on to the present times of the Church. This should be done in such a manner as to give, for each of the affairs and events which we relate, causes and reasons by which we may refer them severally to that end of love from which neither the eye of the man who is occupied in doing anything, nor that of the man who is engaged in speaking, ought to be turned away. For if, even in

handling the fables of the poets, which are but fictitious creations and things devised for the pleasure of minds whose food is found in trifles, those grammarians who have the reputation and the name of being good do nevertheless endeavor to bring them to bear upon some kind of (assumed) use, although that use itself may be only something vain and grossly bent upon the coarse nutriment of this world: how much more careful does it become us to be, not to let those genuine verities which we narrate, in consequence of any want of a well-considered account of their causes, be accepted either with a gratification which issues in no practical good, or, still less, with a cupidity which may prove hurtful! At the same time, we are not to set forth these causes in such a manner as to leave the proper course of our narration, and let our heart and our tongue indulge in digressions into the knotty questions of more intricate discussion. But the simple truth of the explanation which we adduce ought to be like the gold which binds together a row of gems, and yet does not interfere with the choice symmetry of the ornament by any undue intrusion of itself.

Chapter 7. —Of the Exposition of the Resurrection, the Judgment, and Other Subjects, Which Should Follow This Narration.

11. On the completion of this narration, the hope of the resurrection should be set forth, and, so far as the capacity and strength of the hearer will bear it, and so far also as the measure of time at our disposal will allow, we ought to handle our arguments against the vain scoffings of unbelievers on the subject of the resurrection of the body, as well as on that of the future judgment, with its goodness in relation to the good, its severity in relation to the evil, its truth in relation to all. And after the penalties of the impious have thus been declared with detestation and horror, then the kingdom of the righteous and faithful, and that supernal city and its joy, should form the next themes for our discourse. At this point, moreover, we ought to equip and

animate the weakness of man in withstanding temptations and offenses, whether these emerge without or rise within the church itself; without, as in opposition to Gentiles, or Jews, or heretics; within, on the other hand, as in opposition to the chaff of the Lord's threshing-floor. It is not meant, however, that we are to dispute against each several type of perverse men, and that all their wrong opinions are to be refuted by set arrays of argumentations: but, in a manner suitable to a limited allowance of time, we ought to show how all this was foretold, and to point out of what service temptations are in the training of the faithful, and what relief there is in the example of the patience of God, who has resolved to permit them even to the end. But, again, while he is being furnished against these (adversaries), whose perverse multitudes fill the churches so far as bodily presence is concerned, the precepts of a Christian and honorable manner of life should also be briefly and befittingly detailed at the same time, to the intent that he may neither allow himself to be easily led astray in this way, by any who are drunkards, covetous, fraudulent, gamesters, adulterers, fornicators, lovers of public spectacles, wearers of unholy charms, sorcerers, astrologers, or diviners practicing any sort of vain and wicked arts, and all other parties of a similar character; nor to let himself fancy that any such course may be followed with impunity on his part, simply because he sees many who are called Christians loving these things, and engaging themselves with them, and defending them, and recommending them, and actually persuading others to their use. For as to the end which is appointed for those who persist in such a mode of life, and as to the method in which they are to be borne with in the church itself, out of which they are destined to be separated in the end, —these are subjects in which the learner ought to be instructed by means of the testimonies of the divine books. He should also, however, be informed beforehand that he will find in the church many good Christians, most genuine citizens of the heavenly Jerusalem, if he sets about being such himself. And, finally, he must be sedulously warned against letting his hope rest on man. For it is not a matter that can be easily judged by man, what man is righteous. And even were this a matter which could be easily done, still the object with which the examples of righteous men are set before us is not that we may be justified by them, but that, as we imitate them, we may understand how we ourselves also are justified by their Justifier. For the issue of this will be something which must merit the highest approval,—namely this, that when the person who is hearing us, or rather, who is hearing God by us, has begun to make some progress in moral qualities and in knowledge, and to enter upon the way of Christ with ardor, he will not be so bold as to ascribe the change either to us or to himself; but he will love both himself and us, and whatever other persons he loves as friends, in Him, and for His sake who loved him when he was an enemy, in order that He might justify him and make him a friend. And now that we have advanced thus far, I do not think that you need any preceptor to tell you how you should discuss matters briefly, when either your own time or that of those who are hearing you is occupied; and how, on the other hand, you should discourse at greater length when there is more time at your command. For the very necessity of the case recommends this, apart from the counsel of any adviser.

Chapter 8. —Of the Method to Be Pursued in Catechising Those Who Have Had a Liberal Education.

12. But there is another case which evidently must not be overlooked. I mean the case of one coming to you to receive catchetical instruction who has cultivated the field of liberal studies, who has already made up his mind to be a Christian, and who has betaken himself to you for the express purpose of becoming one. It can scarcely fail to be the fact that a person of this character has already acquired a considerable knowledge of our Scriptures and literature; and, furnished with this, he may have come now simply with the view of being made a partaker in the sacraments. For it is customary with men of this class to inquire carefully into all things, not at the very time when they are made

Christians, but previous to that, and thus early also to communicate and reason, with any whom they can reach, on the subject of the feelings of their own minds. Consequently, a brief method of procedure should be adopted with these, so as not to inculcate on them, in an odious fashion things which they know already, but to pass over these with a light and modest touch. Thus, we should say how we believe that they are already familiar with this and the other subject, and that we therefore simply reckon up in a cursory manner all those facts which require to be formally urged upon the attention of the uninstructed and unlearned. And we should endeavor so to proceed, that, supposing this man of culture to have been previously acquainted with any one of our themes, he may not hear it now as from a teacher; and that, in the event of his being still ignorant of any of them, he may yet learn the same while we are going over the things with which we understand him to be already familiar. Moreover, it is certainly not without advantage to interrogate the man himself as to the means by which he was induced to desire to be a Christian; so that, if you discover him to have been moved to that decision by books, whether they be the canonical writings or the compositions of literary men worth the studying, you may say something about these at the outset, expressing your approbation of them in a manner which may suit the distinct merits which they severally possess, in respect of canonical authority and of skillfully applied diligence on the part of these expounders; and, in the case of the canonical Scriptures, commending above all the most salutary modesty (of language) displayed alongside their wonderful loftiness (of subject); while, in those other productions you notice, in accordance with the characteristic faculty of each several writer, a style of a more sonorous and, as it were more rounded eloquence adapted to minds that are prouder, and, by reason thereof weaker. We should certainly also elicit from him some account of himself, so that he may give us to understand what writer he chiefly perused, and with what books he was more familiarly conversant, as these were the means of moving him to wish to be associated with the church. And when he has given us this information, then if the said books are known to us, or if we have at least ecclesiastical report as our warrant for taking them to have been written by some catholic man of note, we should joyfully express our approbation. But if, on the other hand, he has fallen upon the productions of some heretic and in ignorance, it may be, has retained in his mind anything which the true faith condemns, and yet supposes it to be catholic doctrine, then we must set ourselves sedulously to teach him, bringing before him (in its rightful superiority) the authority of the Church universal, and of other most learned men reputed both for their disputations and for their writings in (the cause of) its truth. At the same time, it is to be admitted that even those who have departed this life as genuine Catholics, and have left to posterity some Christian writings, in certain passages of their small works, either in consequence of their failing to be understood, or (as the way is with human infirmity) because they lack ability to pierce into the deeper mysteries with the eye of the mind, and in (pursuing) the semblance of what is true, wander from the truth itself, have proved an occasion to the presumptuous and audacious for constructing and generating some heresy. This, however, is not to be wondered at, when, even in the instance of the canonical writings themselves, where all things have been expressed in the soundest manner, we see how it has happened,—not indeed through merely taking certain passages in a sense different from that which the writer had in view or which is consistent with the truth itself, (for if this were all, who would not gladly pardon human infirmity, when it exhibits a readiness to accept correction?), but by persistently defending, with the bitterest vehemence and in impudent arrogance, opinions which they have taken up in perversity and error,—many have given birth to many pernicious dogmas at the cost of rending the unity of the (Christian) communion. All these subjects we should discuss in modest conference with the individual who makes his approach to the society of the Christian people, not in the character of an uneducated man, as they say, but in that of one who has passed through a finished culture and training in the books of the learned. And in enjoining him to guard against the errors of presumption, we should assume only so much authority as that humility of his, which induced him to come to us, is now felt to admit of. As to other things, moreover, in accordance with the rules of saving doctrine, which require to be narrated or discussed, whether they be matters relating to the faith, or questions bearing on the moral life, or others dealing with temptations, all these should be gone through in the manner which I have indicated, and ought therein to be referred to the more excellent way (already noticed).

Chapter 9. —Of the Method in Which Grammarians and Professional Speakers are to Be Dealt with.

13. There are also some who come from the commonest schools of the grammarians and professional speakers, whom you may not venture to reckon either among the uneducated or among those very learned classes whose minds have been exercised in questions of real magnitude. When such persons, therefore, who appear to be superior to the rest of mankind, so far as the art of speaking is concerned, approach you with the view of becoming Christians, it will be your duty in your communications with them, in a higher degree than in your dealings with those other illiterate hearers, to make it plain that they are to be diligently admonished to clothe themselves with Christian humility, and learn not to despise individuals whom they may discover keeping themselves free from vices of conduct more carefully than from faults of language; and also that they ought not to presume so much as to compare with a pure heart the practiced tongue which they were accustomed even to put in preference. But above all, such persons should be taught to listen to the divine Scriptures, so that they may neither deem solid eloquence to be mean, merely because it is not inflated, nor suppose that the words or deeds of men, of which we read the accounts in those books, involved and covered as they are in carnal wrappings, are not to be drawn forth and unfolded with a view to an

(adequate) understanding of them, but are to be taken merely according to the sound of the letter. And as to this same matter of the utility of the hidden meaning, the existence of which is the reason why they are called also mysteries, the power wielded by these intricacies of enigmatical utterances in the way of sharpening our love for the truth, and shaking off the torpor of weariness, is a thing which the persons in question must have made good to them by actual experience, when some subject which failed to move them when it was placed baldly before them, has its significance elicited by the detailed working out of an allegorical sense. For it is in the highest degree useful to such men to come to know how ideas are to be preferred to words, just as the soul is preferred to the body. And from this, too, it follows that they ought to have the desire to listen to discourses remarkable for their truth, rather than to those which are notable for their eloquence; just as they ought to be anxious to have friends distinguished for their wisdom, rather than those whose chief merit is their beauty. They should also understand that there is no voice for the ears of God save the affection of the soul. For thus they will not act the mocker if they happen to observe any of the prelates and ministers of the Church either calling upon God in language marked by barbarisms and solecisms, or failing in understanding correctly the very words which they are pronouncing, and making confused pauses. It is not meant, of course, that such faults are not to be corrected, so that the people may say "Amen" to something which they plainly understand; but what is intended is, that such things should be piously borne with by those who have come to understand how, as in the forum it is in the sound, so in the church it is in the desire that the grace of speech resides. Therefore, that of the forum may sometimes be called good speech, but never gracious speech. Moreover, with respect to the sacrament which they are about to receive, it is enough for the more intelligent simply to hear what the thing signifies. But with those of slower intellect, it will be necessary to adopt a somewhat more detailed explanation, together with the use of similitudes, to prevent them from despising what they see.

Chapter 10. —Of the Attainment of Cheerfulness in the Duty of Catechising, and of Various Causes Producing Weariness in the Catechumen.

14. At this point you perhaps desiderate some example of the kind of discourse intended, so that I may show you by an actual instance how the things which I have recommended are to be done. This indeed I shall do, so far as by God's help I shall be able. But before proceeding to that, it is my duty, in consistency with what I have promised, to speak of the acquisition of the cheerfulness (to which I have alluded). For about the matter of the rules in accordance with which your discourse should be set forth, in the case of the catechetical instruction of a person who comes with the express view of being made a Christian, I have already made good, as far as has appeared sufficient, the promise which I made. And surely, I am under no obligation at the same time to do myself in this volume that which I enjoin as the right thing to be done. Consequently, if I do that, it will have the value of an overplus. But how can the overplus be super-added by me before I have filled up the measure of what is due? Besides, one thing which I have heard you make the subject of your complaint above all others, is the fact that your discourse seemed to yourself to be poor and spiritless when you were instructing anyone in the Christian name. Now this, I know, results not so much from want of matter to say, with which I am well aware you are sufficiently provided and furnished, or from poverty of speech itself, as rather from weariness of mind. And that may spring either from the cause of which I have already spoken, namely, the fact that our intelligence is better pleased and more thoroughly arrested by that which we perceive in silence in the mind, and that we have no inclination to have our attention called off from it to a noise of words coming far short of representing it; or from the circumstance that even when discourse is pleasant, we have more delight in hearing or reading things which have been

expressed in a superior manner, and which are set forth without any care or anxiety on our part, than in putting together, with a view to the comprehension of others, words suddenly conceived, and leaving it an uncertain issue, on the one hand, whether such terms occur to us as adequately represent the sense, and on the other, whether they be accepted in such a manner as to profit; or yet again, from the consideration that, in consequence of their being now thoroughly familiar to ourselves, and no longer necessary to our own advancement, it becomes irksome to us to be recurring very frequently to those matters which are urged upon the uninstructed, and our mind, as being by this time pretty well matured, moves with no manner of pleasure in the circle of subjects so well-worn, and, as it were, so childish. A sense of weariness is also induced upon the speaker when he has a hearer who remains unmoved, either in that he is actually not stirred by any feeling, or in that he does not indicate by any motion of the body that he understands or that he is pleased with what is said. Not that it is a becoming disposition in us to be greedy of the praises of men, but that the things which we minister are of God; and the more we love those to whom we discourse, the more desirous are we that they should be pleased with the matters which are held forth for their salvation: so that if we do not succeed in this, we are pained, and we are weakened, and become broken-spirited in the midst of our course, as if we were wasting our efforts to no purpose. Sometimes, too, when we are drawn off from some matter which we are desirous to go on with, and the transaction of which was a pleasure to us, or appeared to be more than usually needful, and when we are compelled, either by the command of a person whom we are unwilling to offend, or by the importunity of some parties that we find it impossible to get rid of, to instruct anyone catechetically, in such circumstances we approach a duty for which great calmness is indispensable with minds already perturbed, and grieving at once that we are not permitted to keep that order which we desire to observe in our actions, and that we cannot possibly be competent for all things; and thus out of very heaviness our discourse as it advances is less of an attraction, because, starting from the arid soil of dejection, it goes on less flowingly. Sometimes, too, sadness has taken possession of our heart in consequence of some offense or other, and at that very time we are addressed thus: "Come, speak with this person; he desires to become a Christian." For they who thus address us do it in ignorance of the hidden trouble which is consuming us within. So it happens that, if they are not the persons to whom it befits us to open up our feelings, we undertake with no sense of pleasure what they desire; and then, certainly, the discourse will be languid and unenjoyable which is transmitted through the agitated and fuming channel of a heart in that condition. Consequently, seeing there are so many causes serving to cloud the calm serenity of our minds, in accordance with God's will we must seek remedies for them, such as may bring us relief from these feelings of heaviness, and help us to rejoice in fervor of spirit, and to be jocund in the tranquility of a good work. "For God loveth a cheerful giver."

15. Now if the cause of our sadness lies in the circumstance that our hearer does not apprehend what we mean, so that we have to come down in a certain fashion from the elevation of our own conceptions, and are under the necessity of dwelling long in the tedious processes of syllables which come far beneath the standard of our ideas, and have anxiously to consider how that which we ourselves take in with a most rapid draught of mental apprehension is to be given forth by the mouth of flesh in the long and perplexed intricacies of its method of enunciation; and if the great dissimilarity thus felt (between our utterance and our thought) makes it distasteful to us to speak, and a pleasure to us to keep silence, then let us ponder what has been set before us by Him who has "showed us an example that we should follow His steps." For however much our articulate speech may differ from the vivacity of our intelligence, much greater is the difference of the flesh of mortality from the equality of God. And, neverless, "although He was in the same form, He emptied Himself, taking the form of a servant,"—and so on down to the words "the death of the

cross." What is the explanation of this but that He made Himself "weak to the weak, in order that He might gain the weak?" Listen to His follower as he expresses himself also in another place to this effect: "For whether we be beside ourselves, it is to God; or whether we be sober, it is for your cause. For the love of Christ constrained us, because we thus judge that He died for all." And how, indeed, should one be ready to be spent for their souls, if he should find it irksome to him to bend himself to their ears? For this reason, therefore, He became a little child in the midst of us, (and) like a nurse cherishing her children. For is it a pleasure to lisp shortened and broken words, unless love invites us? And yet men desire to have infants to whom they have to do that kind of service; and it is a sweeter thing to a mother to put small morsels of masticated food into her little son's mouth, than to eat up and devour larger pieces herself. In like manner, accordingly, let not the thought of the hen recede from your heart, who covers her tender brood with her drooping feathers, and with broken voice calls her chirping young ones to her, while they that turn away from her fostering wings in their pride become a prey to birds. For if intelligence brings delights in its purest recesses, it should also be a delight to us to have an intelligent understanding of the manner in which charity, the more complaisantly it descends to the lowest objects, finds its way back, with all the greater vigor to those that are most secret, along the course of a good conscience which witnesses that it has sought nothing from those to whom it has descended except their everlasting salvation.

Chapter 11. —Of the Remedy for the Second Source of Weariness.

16. If, however, it is rather our desire to read or hear such things as are already prepared for our use and expressed in a superior style, and if the consequence is that we feel it irksome to put together, at the time and with an uncertain issue, the terms of discourse on our own side, then, provided only that our mind does not wander off from

the truth of the facts themselves, it is an easy matter for the hearer, if he is offended by anything in our language, to come to see in that very circumstance how little value should be set, supposing the subject itself to be rightly understood, upon the mere fact that there may have been some imperfection or some inaccuracy in the literal expressions, which were employed indeed simply with the view of securing a correct apprehension of the subject-matter. But if the bent of human infirmity has wandered off from the truth of the facts themselves,—although in the catechetical instruction of the unlearned, where we have to keep by the most beaten track, that cannot occur very readily,—still, lest haply it should turn out that our hearer finds cause of offence even in this direction, we ought not to deem this to have come upon us in any other way than as the issue of God's own wish to put us to the test with respect to our readiness to receive correction in calmness of mind, so as not to rush headlong, in the course of a still greater error, into the defense of our error. But if, again, no one has told us of it, and if the thing has altogether escaped our own notice, as well as the observation of our hearers, then there is nothing to grieve over, provided only the same thing does not occur a second time. For the most part, however, when we recall what we have said, we ourselves discover something to find fault with, and are ignorant of the manner in which it was received when it was uttered; and so when charity is fervent within us, we are the more vexed if the thing, while really false, has been received with unquestioning acceptance. This being the case, then, whenever an opportunity occurs, as we have been finding fault with ourselves in silence, we ought in like manner to see to it that those persons be also set right on the subject in a considerate method, who have fallen into some sort of error, not by the words of God, but plainly by those used by us. If, on the other hand, there are any who, blinded by insensate spite, rejoice that we have committed a mistake, whisperers as they are, and slanderers, and "hateful to God," such characters should afford us matter for the exercise of patience with pity, inasmuch as also the "patience of God leaded them to repentance." For what is more detestable, and what more likely to "treasure up wrath in the day of wrath and revelation of the righteous judgment of God," than to rejoice, after the evil likeness and pattern of the devil, in the evil of another? At times, too, even when all is correctly and truly spoken, either something which has not been understood, or something which, as being opposed to the idea and wont of an old error, seems harsh in its very novelty, offends and disturbs the hearer. But if this becomes apparent, and if the person shows himself capable of being set right, he should be set right without any delay by the use of abundance of authorities and reasons. On the other hand, if the offense is tacit and hidden, the medicine of God is the effective remedy for it. And if, again, the person starts back and declines to be cured, we should comfort ourselves with that example of our Lord, who, when men were offended at His word, and shrank from it as a hard saying, addressed Himself at the same time to those who had remained, in these terms, "Will ye also go away?" For it ought to be retained as a thoroughly "fixed and immovable" position in our heart, that Jerusalem which is in captivity is set free from the Babylon of this world when the times have run their course, and that none belonging to her shall perish: for whoever may perish was not of her. "For the foundation of God standeth sure, having this seal, The Lord knoweth them that are His; and, let everyone that named the name of Christ depart from iniquity." If we ponder these things, and call upon the Lord to come into our heart, we shall be less apprehensive of the uncertain issues of our discourse, consequent on the uncertain feelings of our hearers; and the very endurance of vexations in the cause of a work of mercy will also be something pleasant to us, if we seek not our own glory in the same. For then is a work truly good, when the aim of the doer gets its impetus from charity, and, as if returning to its own place, rests again in charity. Moreover, the reading which delights us, or any listening to an eloquence superior to our own, the effect of which is to make us inclined to set a greater value upon it than upon the discourse which we ourselves have to deliver, and so to lead us to speak with a reluctant or tedious utterance, will come upon us in a happier spirit, and will be found to be more enjoyable after labor. Then, too, with a stronger confidence shall we pray to God to speak to us as we wish, if we cheerfully submit to let Him speak by us as we are able. Thus, is it brought about that all things come together for good to them that love God.

Chapter 12. —Of the Remedy for the Third Source of Weariness.

17. Once more, however, we often feel it very wearisome to go over repeatedly matters which are thoroughly familiar, and adapted (rather) to children. If this is the case with us, then we should endeavor to meet them with a brother's, a father's, and a mother's love; and, if we are once united with them thus in heart, to us no less than to them will these things seem new. For so great is the power of a sympathetic disposition of mind, that, as they are affected while we are speaking, and we are affected while they are learning, we have our dwelling in each other; and thus, at one and the same time, they as it were in us speak what they hear, and we in them learn after a certain fashion what we teach. Is it not a common occurrence with us, that when we show to persons, who have never seen them, certain spacious and beautiful tracts, either in cities or in fields, which we have been in the habit of passing by without any sense of pleasure, simply because we have become so accustomed to the sight of them, we find our own enjoyment renewed in their enjoyment of the novelty of the scene? And this is so much the more our experience in proportion to the intimacy of our friendship with them; because, just as we are in them in virtue of the bond of love, in the same degree do things become new to us which previously were old. But if we ourselves have made any considerable progress in the contemplative study of things, it is not our wish that those whom we love should simply be gratified and astonished as they gaze upon the works of men's hands; but it becomes our wish to lift them to (the contemplation of) the very skill

or wisdom of their author, and from this to (see them) rise to the admiration and praise of the all-creating God, with whom is the most fruitful end of love. How much more, then, ought we to be delighted when men come to us with the purpose already formed of obtaining the knowledge of God Himself, with a view to (the knowledge of) whom all things should be learned which are to be learned! And how ought we to feel ourselves renewed in their newness (of experience), so that if our ordinary preaching is somewhat frigid, it may rise to fresh warmth under (the stimulus of) their extraordinary hearing! There is also this additional consideration to help us in the attainment of gladness, namely, that we ponder and bear in mind out of what death of error the man is passing over into the life of faith. And if we walk through streets which are most familiar to us, with a beneficent cheerfulness, when we happen to be pointing out the way to some individual who had been in distress in consequence of missing his direction, how much more should be the alacrity of spirit, and how much greater the joy with which, in the matter of saving doctrine, we ought to traverse again and again even those tracks which, so far as we are ourselves concerned, there is no need to open up any more; seeing that we are leading a miserable soul, and one worn out with the devious courses of this world, through the paths of peace, at the command of Him who made that peace good to us!

Chapter 13. —Of the Remedy for the Fourth Source of Weariness.

18. But in good truth it is a serious demand to make upon us, to continue discoursing on to the set limit when we fail to see our hearer in any degree moved; whether it be that, under the restraints of the awe of religion, he has not the boldness to signify his approval by voice or by any movement of his body, or that he is kept back by the modesty proper to man, or that he does not understand our sayings, or that he counts them of no value. Since, then, this must be a matter of uncertainty to us, as we cannot discern

his mind, it becomes our duty in our discourse to make trial of all things which may be of any avail in stirring him up and drawing him forth as it were from his place of concealment. For that sort of fear which is excessive, and which obstructs the declaration of his judgment, ought to be dispelled by the force of kindly exhortation; and by bringing before him the consideration of our brotherly affinity, we should temper his reverence for us; and by questioning him, we should ascertain whether he understands what is addressed to him; and we should impart to him a sense of confidence, so that he may give free expression to any objection which suggests itself to him. We should at the same time ask him whether he has already listened to such themes on some previous occasion, and whether perchance they fail to move him now in consequence of their being to him like things well known and commonplace. And we ought to shape our course in accordance with his answer, so as either to speak in a simpler style and with greater detail of explanation, or to refute some antagonistic opinion, or, instead of attempting any more diffuse exposition of the subjects which are known to him, to give a brief summary of these, and to select some of those matters which are handled in a mystical manner in the holy books, and especially in the historical narrative, the unfolding and setting forth of which may make our addresses more attractive. But if the man is of a very sluggish disposition, and if he is senseless, and without anything in common with all such sources of pleasure, then we must simply bear with him in a compassionate spirit; and, after briefly going over other points, we ought to impress upon him, in a manner calculated to inspire him with awe, the truths which are most indispensable on the subject of the unity of the Catholic Church, on that of temptation, on that of a Christian conversation in view of the future judgment; and we ought rather to address ourselves to God for him than address much to him concerning God.

19. It is likewise a frequent occurrence that one who at first listened to us with all readiness, becomes exhausted either by the effort of hearing or by standing, and now no

longer commends what is said, but gapes and yawns, and even unwillingly exhibits a disposition to depart. When we observe that, it becomes our duty to refresh his mind by saying something seasoned with an honest cheerfulness and adapted to the matter which is being discussed, or something of a very wonderful and amazing order, or even, it may be, something of a painful and mournful nature. Whatever we thus say may be all the better if it affects himself more immediately, so that the quick sense of self-concern may keep his attention on the alert. At the same time, however, it should not be of the kind to offend his spirit of reverence by any harshness attaching to it; but it should be of a nature fitted rather to conciliate him by the friendliness which it breathes. Or else, we should relieve him by accommodating him with a seat, although unquestionably matters will be better ordered if from the outset, whenever that can be done with propriety, he sits and listens. And indeed, in certain of the churches beyond the sea, with a far more considerate regard to the fitness of things, not only do the prelates sit when they address the people, but they also themselves put down seats for the people, lest any person of enfeebled strength should become exhausted by standing, and thus have his mind diverted from the most wholesome purport (of the discourse), or even be under the necessity of departing. And yet it is one thing if it be simply someone out of a great multitude who withdraws in order to recruit his strength, he being also already under the obligations which result from participation in the sacraments; and it is quite another thing if the person withdrawing is one (inasmuch as it is usually the case in these circumstances that the man is unavoidably urged to that course by the fear that he should even fall, overcome by internal weakness) who has to be initiated in the first sacraments; for a person in this position is at once restrained by the sense of shame from stating the reason of his going, and not permitted to stand through the force of his weakness. This I speak from experience. For this was the case with a certain individual, a man from the country, when I was instructing him catechetically: and from his instance I have learned that this kind of thing is carefully to be guarded against. For who can endure our arrogance when we fail to make men who are our brethren, or even those who are not yet in that relation to us (for our solicitude then should be all the greater to get them to become our brethren), to be seated in our presence, seeing that even a woman sat as she listened to our Lord Himself, in whose service the angels stand alert? Of course, if the address is to be but short, or if the place is not well adapted for sitting, they should listen standing. But that should be the case only when there are many hearers, and when they are not to be formally admitted at the time. For when the audience consists only of one or two, or a few, who have come with the express purpose of being made Christians, there is a risk in speaking to them standing. Nevertheless, supposing that we have once begun in that manner, we ought at least, whenever we observe signs of weariness on the part of the hearer, to offer him the liberty of being seated; nay more, we should urge him by all means to sit down, and we ought to drop some remark calculated at once to refresh him and to banish from his mind any anxiety which may have chanced to break in upon him and draw off his attention. For inasmuch as the reasons why he remains silent and declines to listen cannot be certainly known to us, now that he is seated we may speak to some extent against the incidence of thoughts about worldly affairs, delivering ourselves either in the cheerful spirit to which I have already adverted, or in a serious vein; so that, if these are the particular anxieties which have occupied his mind, they may be made to give way as if indicted by name: while, on the other hand, supposing them not to be the special causes (of the loss of interest), and supposing him to be simply worn out with listening, his attention will be relieved of the pressure of weariness when we address to him some unexpected and extraordinary strain of remark on these subjects, in the mode of which I have spoken, as if they were the particular anxieties,—for indeed we are simply ignorant (of the true causes). But let the remark thus made be short, especially considering that it is thrown in out of order, lest the very medicine even increase the malady of weariness which we desire to relieve; and, at the same time, we should go on rapidly with what remains, and promise and present the prospect of a conclusion nearer than was looked for.

Chapter 14. —Of the Remedy Against the Fifth and Sixth Sources of Weariness.

20. If, again, your spirit has been broken by the necessity of giving up some other employment, on which, as the more requisite, you were now bent; and if the sadness caused by that constraint makes you catechise in no pleasant mood, you ought to ponder the fact that, excepting that we know it to be our duty, in all our dealings with men, to act in a merciful manner, and in the exercise of the sincerest charity,—with this one exception, I say, it is quite uncertain to us what is the more profitable thing for us to do, and what the more opportune thing for us either to pass by for a time or altogether to omit. For inasmuch as we know not how the merits of men, on whose behalf we are acting, stand with God, the question as to what is expedient for them at a certain time is something which, instead of being able to comprehend, we can rather only surmise, without the aid of any (clear) inferences, or (at best) with the slenderest and the most uncertain. Therefore, we ought certainly to dispose the matters with which we have to deal according to our intelligence; and then, if we prove able to carry them out in the manner upon which we have resolved, we should rejoice, not indeed that it was our will, but that it was God's will, that they should thus be accomplished. But if anything unavoidable happens, by which the disposition thus proposed by us is interfered with, we should bend ourselves to it readily, lest we be broken; so that the very disposition of affairs which God has preferred to ours may also be made our own. For it is more in accordance with propriety that we should follow His will than that He should follow ours. Besides, as regards this order in the doing of things, which we wish to keep in accordance with our own judgment, surely that course is to be approved of in which objects that

are superior have the precedence. Why then are we aggrieved that the precedence over men should be held by the Lord God in His vast superiority to us men, so that in the said love which we entertain for our own order, we should thus (exhibit the disposition to) despise order? For "no one orders for the better" what he has to do, except the man who is rather ready to leave undone what he is prohibited from doing by the divine power, than desirous of doing that which he meditates in his own human cogitations. For "there are many devices in a man's heart; nevertheless, the counsel of the Lord stands forever."

21. But if our mind is agitated by some cause of offense, so as not to be capable of delivering a discourse of a calm and enjoyable strain, our charity towards those for whom Christ died, desiring to redeem them by the price of His own blood from the death of the errors of this world, ought to be so great, that the very circumstance of intelligence being brought us in our sadness, regarding the advent of some person who longs to become a Christian, ought to be enough to cheer us and dissipate that heaviness of spirit, just as the delights of gain are wont to soften the pain of losses. For we are not (fairly) oppressed by the offense of any individual, unless it be that of the man whom we either perceive or believe to be perishing himself, or to be the occasion of the undoing of some weak one. Accordingly, one who comes to us with the view of being formally admitted, in that we cherish the hope of his ability to go forward, should wipe away the sorrow caused by one who fails us. For even if the dread that our proselyte may become the child of hell comes into our thoughts, as, there are many such before our eyes, from whom those offenses arise by which we are distressed, this ought to operate, not in the way of keeping us back, but rather in the way of stimulating us and spurring us on. And in the same measure we ought to admonish him whom we are instructing to be on his guard against imitating those who are Christians only in name and not in very truth, and to take care not to suffer himself to be so moved by their numbers as either to be desirous of following them, or to be reluctant to follow Christ on their

account, and either to be unwilling to be in the Church of God, where they are, or to wish to be there in such a character as they bear. And somehow or other, in admonitions of this sort, that address is the more glowing to which a present sense of grief supplies the fuel; so that instead of being duller, we utter with greater fire and vehemence under such feelings things which, in times of greater ease, we would give forth in a colder and less energetic manner. And this should make us rejoice that an opportunity is afforded us under which the emotions of our mind pass not away without yielding some fruit.

22. If, however, grief has taken possession of us because something in which we ourselves have erred or sinned, we should bear in mind not only that a "broken spirit is a sacrifice to God," but also the saying, "Like as water quenches fire, so alms sin;" and again, "I will have mercy," saith He, "rather than sacrifice." Therefore, as in the event of our being in peril from fire we would certainly run to the water in order to get the fire extinguished, and we would be grateful if any person were to offer it in the immediate vicinity; so, if some flame of sin has risen from our own stack, and if we are troubled on that account, when an opportunity has been given for a most merciful work, we should rejoice in it, as if a fountain were offered us in order that by it the conflagration which had burst forth might be extinguished. Unless haply we are foolish enough to think that we ought to be readier in running with bread, wherewith we may fill the belly of a hungry man, than with the word of God, wherewith we may instruct the mind of the man who feeds on it. There is this also to consider, namely, that if it would only be of advantage to us to do this thing, and entail no disadvantage to leave it undone, we might despise a remedy offered in an unhappy fashion in the time of peril with a view to the safety, not now of a neighbor, but of ourselves. But when from the mouth of the Lord this so threatening sentence is heard, "Thou wicked and slothful servant, thou oughtest to give my money to the exchangers," what madness, I pray thee, is it thus, seeing that our sin pains us, to be minded to sin again, by refusing to give the

Lord's money to one who desires it and asks it! When these and such like considerations and reflections have succeeded in dispelling the darkness of weary feelings, the bent of mind is rendered apt for the duty of catechising, so that that is received in a pleasant manner which breaks forth vigorously and cheerfully from the rich vein of charity. For these things indeed which are uttered here are spoken, not so much by me to you, as rather to us all by that very "love which is shed abroad in our hearts by the Holy Spirit that is given to us."

Chapter 15. —Of the Method in Which Our Address Should Be Adapted to Different Classes of Hearers.

23. But now, perhaps, you also demand of me as a debt that which, previous to the promise which I made, I was under no obligation to give, namely, that I should not count it burdensome to unfold some sort of example of the discourse intended, and to set it before you for your study, just as if I were myself engaged in catechising some individual. Before I do that, however, I wish you to keep in mind the fact that the mental effort is of one kind in the case of a person who dictates, with a future reader in his view, and that it is of quite another kind in the case of a person who speaks with a present hearer to whom to direct his attention. And further, it is to be remembered that, in this latter instance in particular, the effort is of one kind when one is admonishing in private, and when there is no other person at hand to pronounce judgment on us; whereas it is of a different order when one is conveying any instruction in public, and when there stands around him an audience of persons holding dissimilar opinions; and again, that in this exercise of teaching, the effort will be of one sort when only a single individual is being instructed, while all the rest listen, like persons judging or attesting things well known to them, and that it will be different when all those who are present wait for what we have to deliver to them; and once more, that, in this same instance, the effort will be one thing when all are seated, as it were, in private conference with a

view to engaging in some discussion, and that it will be quite another thing when the people sit silent and intent on giving their attention to some single speaker who is to address them from a higher position. It will likewise make a considerable difference, even when we are discoursing in that style, whether there are few present or many, whether they are learned or unlearned, or made up of both classes combined; whether they are city-bred or rustics, or both the one and the other together; or whether, again, they are a people composed of all orders of men in due proportion. For it is impossible but that they will affect in different ways the person who has to speak to them and discourse with them, and that the address which is delivered will both bear certain features, as it were, expressive of the feelings of the mind from which it proceeds, and also influence the hearers in different ways, in accordance with that same difference (in the speaker's disposition), while at the same time the hearers themselves will influence one another in different ways by the simple force of their presence with each other. But as we are dealing at present with the matter of the instruction of the unlearned, I am a witness to you, as regards my own experience, that I find myself variously moved, according as I see before me, for the purposes of catechetical instruction, a highly educated man, a dull fellow, a citizen, a foreigner, a rich man, a poor man, a private individual, a man of honors, a person occupying some position of authority, an individual of this or the other nation, of this or the other age or sex, one proceeding from this or the other sect, from this or the other common error,—and ever in accordance with the difference of my feelings does my discourse itself at once set out, go on, and reach its end. And inasmuch as, although the same charity is due to all, yet the same medicine is not to be administered to all, in like manner charity itself travails with some, is made weak together with others; is at pains to edify some, tremblingly apprehends being an offense to others; bends to some, lifts itself erect to others; is gentle to some, severe to others; to none an enemy, to all a mother. And when one, who has not gone through the kind of experience to which I refer in the same spirit of charity, sees us attaining, in virtue of some gift which has been conferred upon us, and which carries the power of pleasing, a certain repute of an eulogistic nature in the mouth of the multitude, he counts us happy on that account. But may God, into whose cognizance the "groaning of them that are bound enters," look upon our humility, and our labor, and forgive us all our sins. Wherefore, if anything in us has so far pleased you as to make you desirous of hearing from us some remarks on the subject of the form of discourse which you ought to follow, you should acquire a more thorough understanding of the matter by contemplating us, and listening to us when we are actually engaged with these topics, than by a perusal when we are only dictating them.

Chapter 16. —A Specimen of a Catechetical Address; And First, the Case of a Catechumen with Worthy Views.

24. Nevertheless, however that may be, let us here suppose that someone has come to us who desires to be made a Christian, and who belongs indeed to the order of private persons, and yet not to the class of rustics, but to that of the city-bred, such as those whom you cannot fail to come across in numbers in Carthage. Let us also suppose that, on being asked whether the inducement leading him to desire to be a Christian is any advantage looked for in the present life, or the rest which is hoped for after this life, he has answered that his inducement has been the rest that is yet to come. Then perchance such a person might be instructed by us in some such strain of address as the following: "Thanks be to God, my brother; cordially do I wish you joy, and I am glad on your account that, amid all the storms of this world, which are at once so great and so dangerous, you have bethought yourself of some true and certain security. For even in this life men go in quest of rest and security at the cost of heavy labors, but they fail to find such in consequence of their wicked lusts. For their thought is to find rest in things which are unquiet, and which endure not. And these objects, inasmuch as they are withdrawn

from them and pass away in the course of time, agitate them by fears and griefs, and suffer them not to enjoy tranquility. For if it be that a man seeks to find his rest in wealth, he is rendered proud rather than at ease. Do we not see how many have lost their riches on a sudden, —how many, too, have been undone by reason of them, either as they have been coveting to possess them, or as they have been borne down and despoiled of them by others more covetous than themselves? And even should they remain with the man all his life long, and never leave their lover, yet would he himself (have to) leave them at his death. For of what measure is the life of man, even if he lives to old age? Or when men desire for themselves old age, what else do they really desire but long infirmity? So, too, with the honors of this world, —what are they but empty pride and vanity, and peril of ruin? For holy Scripture speaks in this wise: 'All flesh is grass, and the glory of man is as the flower of grass. The grass withered, the flower thereof falleth away; but the word of the Lord endures forever.' Consequently, if any man longs for true rest and true felicity, he ought to lift his hope off things which are mortal and transitory, and fix it on the word of the Lord; so that, cleaving to that which endures forever, he may himself together with it endure forever.

25. "There are also other men who neither crave to be rich nor go about seeking the vain pomps of honors, but who nevertheless are minded to find their pleasure and rest in dainty meats, and in fornications, and in those theatres and spectacles which are at their disposal in great cities for nothing. But it fares with these, too, in the same way; or they waste their small means in luxury, and subsequently, under pressure of want, break out into thefts and burglaries, and at times even into highway robberies, and so they are suddenly filled with fears both numerous and great; and men who a little before were singing in the house of revelry, are now dreaming of the sorrows of the prison. Moreover, in their eager devotion to the public spectacles, they come to resemble demons, as they incite men by their cries to wound each other, and instigate those who have done them no hurt to engage in furious contests with each other, while they

seek to please an insane people. And if they perceive any such to be peaceably disposed, they straightway hate them and persecute them, and raise an outcry, asking that they should be beaten with clubs, as if they had been in collusion to cheat them; and this iniquity they force even the judge, who is the (appointed) avenger of iniquities, to perpetrate. On the other hand, if they observe such men exerting themselves in horrid hostilities against each other, whether they be those who are called sintœ, or theatrical actors and players, or charioteers, or hunters,—those wretched men whom they engage in conflicts and struggles, not only men with men, but even men with beasts,—then the fiercer the fury with which they perceive these unhappy creatures rage against each other, the better they like them, and the greater the enjoyment they have in them; and they favor them when thus excited, and by so favoring them they excite them all the more, the spectators themselves striving more madly with each other, as they espouse the cause of different combatants, than is the case even with those very men whose madness they madly provoke, while at the same time they also long to be spectators of the same in their mad frenzy. How then can that mind keep the soundness of peace which feeds on strifes and contentions? For just as is the food which is received, such is the health which results. In fine, although mad pleasures are no pleasures, nevertheless let these things be taken as they are, and it still remains the case that, whatever their nature may be, and whatever the measure of enjoyment yielded by the boasts of riches, and the inflation of honors, and the spendthrift pleasures of the taverns, and the contests of the theatres, and the impurity of fornications, and the pruriency of the baths, they are all things of which one little fever deprives us, while, even from those who still survive, it takes away the whole false happiness of their life. Then there remains only a void and wounded conscience, destined to apprehend that God as a Judge whom it refused to have as a Father, and destined also to find a severe Lord in Him whom it scorned to seek and love as a tender Father. But thou, inasmuch as thou seekest that true rest which is promised to Christians after this life, wilt taste the same sweet and pleasant rest even here among the bitterest troubles of this life, if thou continues to love the commandments of Him who hath promised the same. For quickly wilt thou feel that the fruits of righteousness are sweeter than those of unrighteousness, and that a man finds a more genuine and pleasurable joy in the possession of a good conscience in the midst of troubles than in that of an evil conscience in the midst of delights. For thou hast not come to be united to the Church of God with the idea of seeking from it any temporal advantage.

Chapter 17. —The Specimen of Catechetical Discourse Continued, in Reference Specially to the Reproval of False Aims on the Catechumen's Part.

26. "For there are some whose reason for desiring to become Christians is either that they may gain the favor of men from whom they look for temporal advantages, or that they are reluctant to offend those whom they fear. But these are reprobate; and although the church bears them for a time, as the threshing-floor bears the chaff until the period of winnowing, yet if they fail to amend and begin to be Christians in sincerity in view of the everlasting rest which is to come, they will be separated from it in the end. And let not such flatter themselves, because it is possible for them to be in the threshing-floor along with the grain of God. For they will not be together with that in the barn, but are destined for the fire, which is their due. There are also others of better hope indeed, but nevertheless in no inferior danger. I mean those who now fear God, and mock not the Christian name, neither enter the church of God with an assumed heart, but still look for their felicity in this life, expecting to have more felicity in earthly things than those enjoy who refuse to worship God. And the consequence of this false anticipation is, that when they see some wicked and impious men strongly established and excelling in this worldly prosperity, while they themselves either possess it in a smaller degree or miss it altogether, they are troubled with the thought that they are serving God without reason, and so

they readily fall away from the faith.

27. "But as to the man who has in view that everlasting blessedness and perpetual rest which is promised as the lot destined for the saints after this life, and who desires to become a Christian, in order that he may not pass into eternal fire with the devil, but enter into the eternal kingdom together with Christ, such an one is truly a Christian; (and he will be) on his guard in every temptation, so that he may neither be corrupted by prosperity nor be utterly broken in spirit by adversity, but remain at once modest and temperate when the good things of earth abound with him, and brave and patient when tribulations overtake him. A person of this character will also advance in attainments until he comes to that disposition of mind which will make him love God more than he fears hell; so that even were God to say to him, 'Avail yourself of carnal pleasures forever, and sin as much as you are able, and you shall neither die nor be sent into hell, but you will only not be with me, he would be terribly dismayed, and would altogether abstain from sinning, not now (simply) with the purpose of not falling into that of which he was wont to be afraid, but with the wish not to offend Him whom he so greatly loves: in whom alone also there is the rest which eye hath not seen, neither hath ear heard, neither hath it entered into the heart of man (to conceive),—the rest which God hath prepared for them that love Him.

28. "Now, on the subject of this rest Scripture is significant, and refrains not to speak, when it tells us how at the beginning of the world, and at the time when God made heaven and earth and all things which are in them, He worked during six days, and rested on the seventh day. For it was in the power of the Almighty to make all things even in one moment of time. For He had not labored in the view that He might enjoy (a needful) rest, since indeed "He spoke, and they were made; He commanded, and they were created;" but that He might signify how, after six ages of this world, in a seventh age, as on the seventh day, He will rest in His saints; inasmuch as these same saints shall rest also in Him after all the good works in which they have served

Him,—which He Himself, indeed, works in them, who calls them, and instructs them, and puts away the offenses that are past, and justifies the man who previously was ungodly. For as, when by His gift they work that which is good, He is Himself rightly said to work (that in them), so, when they rest in Him, He is rightly said to rest Himself. For, as regards Himself, He seeks no cessation, because He feels no labor. Moreover, He made all things by His Word; and His Word is Christ Himself, in whom the angels and all those purest spirits of heaven rest in holy silence. Man, however in that he fell by sin, has lost the rest which he possessed in His divinity, and receives it again (now) in His humanity; and for this purpose He became man, and was born of a woman, at the seasonable time at which He Himself knew it behooved it so to be fulfilled. And from the flesh assuredly He could not sustain any contamination, being Himself rather destined to purify the flesh. Of His future coming the ancient saints, in the revelation of the Spirit, had knowledge, and prophesied. And thus were they saved by believing that He was to come, even as we are saved by believing that He has come. Hence ought we to love God who has so loved us as to have sent His only Son, in order that He might endue Himself with the lowliness of our mortality, and die both at the hands of sinners and on behalf of sinners. For even in times of old, and in the opening ages, the depth of this mystery ceases not to be prefigured and prophetically announced.

Chapter 18. —Of What is to Be Believed on the Subject of the Creation of Man and Other Objects.

29. "Whereas, then, the omnipotent God, who is also good and just and merciful, who made all things,—whether they be great or small, whether they be highest or lowest, whether they be things which are seen, such as are the heavens and the earth and the sea, and in the heavens, in particular, the sun and the moon and other luminaries, and in the earth and the sea, again, trees and shrubs and animals each after their kind, and all bodies celestial or terrestrial

alike, or whether they be things which are not seen, such as are those spirits whereby bodies are animated and endowed with life,—made also man after His own image, in order that, as He Himself, in virtue of His omnipotence, presides over universal creation, so man, in virtue of that intelligence of his by which he comes to know even his Creator and worships Him, might preside over all the living creatures of earth: Whereas, too, he made the woman to be an helpmeet for him: not for carnal concupiscence,—since, indeed, they had not corruptible bodies at that period, before the punishment of sin invaded them in the form of mortality,— but for this purpose, that the man might at once have glory of the woman in so far as he went before her to God, and present in himself an example to her for imitation in holiness and piety, even as he himself was to be the glory of God in so far as he followed his wisdom:

    30. "Therefore did he place them in a certain locality of perpetual blessedness, which the Scripture designates Paradise: and he gave them a commandment, on condition of not violating which they were to continue forever in that blessedness of immortality; while, on the other hand, if they transgressed it, they were to sustain the penalties of mortality. Now God knew beforehand that they would transgress it. Nevertheless, in that He is the author and maker of everything good, He chose rather to make them, as He also made the beasts, in order that He might replenish the earth with the good things proper to earth. And certainly man, even sinful man, is better than a beast. And the commandment, which they were not to keep, He yet preferred to give them, in order that they might be without excuse when He should begin to vindicate Himself against them. For whatever man may have done, he finds God worthy to be praised in all His doings: if he shall have acted rightly, he finds Him worthy to be praised for the righteousness of His rewards: if he shall have sinned, he finds Him worthy to be praised for the righteousness of His punishments: if he shall have confessed his sins and returned to an upright life, he finds Him worthy to be praised for the mercy of His pardoning favors. Why, then,

should God not make man, although He foreknew that he would sin, when He might crown him if he stood, and set him right if he fell, and help him if he rose, Himself being always and everywhere glorious in goodness, righteousness, and clemency? Above all, why should He not do so, since He also foreknew this, namely, that from the race of that mortality there would spring saints, who should not seek their own, but give glory to their Creator; and who, obtaining deliverance from every corruption by worshipping Him, should be counted worthy to live forever, and to live in blessedness with the holy angels? For He who gave freedom of will to men, in order that they might worship God not of slavish necessity but with ingenuous inclination, gave it also to the angels; and hence neither did the angel, who, in company with other spirits who were his satellites, forsook in pride the obedience of God and became the devil, do any hurt to God, but to himself. For God knoweth how to dispose of souls that leave Him, and out of their righteous misery to furnish the inferior sections of His creatures with the most appropriate and befitting laws of His wonderful dispensation. Consequently, neither did the devil in any manner harm God, whether in falling himself, or in seducing man to death; nor did man himself in any degree impair the truth, or power, or blessedness of His Maker, in that, when his partner was seduced by the devil, he of his own deliberate inclination consented unto her in the doing of that which God had forbidden. For by the most righteous laws of God all were condemned, God Himself being glorious in the equity of retribution, while they were shamed through the degradation of punishment: to the end that man, when he turned away from his Creator, should be overcome by the devil and made his subject, and that the devil might be set before man as an enemy to be conquered, when he turned again to his Creator; so that whosoever should consent unto the devil even to the end, might go with him into eternal punishments; whereas those who should humble themselves to God, and by His grace overcome the devil, might be counted worthy of eternal rewards.

Chapter 19. —Of the Co-Existence of Good and Evil in the Church, and Their Final Separation.

31. "Neither ought we to be moved by the consideration that many consent unto the devil, and few follow God; for the grain, too, in comparison with the chaff, has greatly the defect in number. But even as the husbandman knows what to do with the mighty heap of chaff, so the multitude of sinners is nothing to God, who knows what to do with them, so as not to let the administration of His kingdom be disordered and dishonored in any part. Nor is the devil to be supposed to have proved victorious for the mere reason of his drawing away with him more than the few by whom he may be overcome. In this way there are two communities—one of the ungodly, and another of the holy—which are carried down from the beginning of the human race even to the end of the world, which are at present commingled in respect of bodies, but separated in respect of wills, and which, moreover, are destined to be separated also in respect of bodily presence in the day of judgment. For all men who love pride and temporal power with vain elation and pomp of arrogance, and all spirits who set their affections on such things and seek their own glory in the subjection of men, are bound fast together in one association; nay, even although they frequently fight against each other on account of these things, they are nevertheless precipitated by the like weight of lust into the same abyss, and are united with each other by similarity of manners and merits. And, again, all men and all spirits who humbly seek the glory of God and not their own, and who follow Him in piety, belong to one fellowship. And, notwithstanding this, God is most merciful and patient with ungodly men, and offers them a place for penitence and amendment.

32. "For with respect also to the fact that He destroyed all men in the flood, with the exception of one righteous man together with his house, whom He willed to

be saved in the ark, He knew indeed that they would not amend themselves; yet, nevertheless, as the building of the ark went on for the space of a hundred years, the wrath of God which was to come upon them was certainly preached to them: and if they only would have turned to God, He would have spared them, as at a later period He spared the city of Nineveh when it repented, after He had announced to it, by means of a prophet, the destruction that was about to overtake it. Thus, moreover, God acts, granting a space for repentance even to those who He knows will persist in wickedness, in order that He may exercise and instruct our patience by His own example; whereby also we may know how greatly it befits us to bear with the evil in long-suffering, when we know not what manner of men they will prove hereafter, seeing that He, whose cognizance nothing that is yet to be escapes, spares them and suffers them to live. Under the sacramental sign of the flood, however, in which the righteous were rescued by the wood, there was also a fore-announcement of the Church which was to be, which Christ, its King and God, has raised on high; by the mystery of His cross, in safety from the submersion of this world. Moreover, God was not ignorant of the fact that, even of those who had been saved in the ark, there would be born wicked men, who would cover the face of the earth a second time with iniquities. But, nevertheless, He both gave them a pattern of the future judgment, and fore-announced the deliverance of the holy by the mystery of the wood. For even after these things wickedness did not cease to sprout forth again through pride, and lusts, and illicit impieties, when men, forsaking their Creator, not only fell to the (standard of the) creature which God made, so as to worship instead of God that which God made, but even bowed their souls to the works of the hands of men and to the contrivances of craftsmen, wherein a more shameful triumph was to be won over them by the devil, and by those evil spirits who rejoice in finding themselves adored and reverenced in such false devices, while they feed their own errors with the errors of men.

  33. "But in truth there were not wanting in those

times righteous men also of the kind to seek God piously and to overcome the pride of the devil, citizens of that holy community, who were made whole by the humiliation of Christ, which was then only destined to enter, but was revealed to them by the Spirit. From among these, Abraham, a pious and faithful servant of God, was chosen, in order that to him might be shown the sacrament of the Son of God, so that thus, in virtue of the imitation of his faith, all the faithful of all nations might be called his children in the future. Of him was born a people, by whom the one true God who made heaven and earth should be worshipped when all other nations did service to idols and evil spirits. In that people, plainly, the future Church was much more evidently prefigured. For in it there was a carnal multitude that worshipped God with a view to visible benefits. But in it there were also a few who thought of the future rest, and looked longingly for the heavenly fatherland, to whom through prophecy was revealed the coming humiliation of God in the person of our King and Lord Jesus Christ, in order that they might be made whole of all pride and arrogance through that faith. And with respect to these saints who in point of time had precedence of the birth of the Lord, not only their speech, but also their life, and their marriages, and their children, and their doings, constituted a prophecy of this time, at which the Church is being gathered together out of all nations through faith in the passion of Christ. By the instrumentality of those holy patriarchs and prophets this carnal people of Israel, who at a later period were also called Jews, had ministered unto them at once those visible benefits which they eagerly desired of the Lord in a carnal manner, and those chastisements, in the form of bodily punishments, which were intended to terrify them for the time, as was befitting for their obstinacy. And in all these, nevertheless, there were also spiritual mysteries signified, such as were meant to bear upon Christ and the Church; of which Church those saints also were members, although they existed in this life previous to the birth of Christ, the Lord, according to the flesh. For this same Christ, the only-begotten Son of God, the Word of the Father, equal and co-eternal with the Father, by whom all things were made, was Himself also made man for our sakes, in order that of the whole Church, as of His whole body, He might be the Head. But just as when the whole man is in the process of being born, although he may put the hand forth first in the act of birth, yet is that hand joined and compacted together with the whole body under the head, even as also among these same patriarchs some were born with the hand put forth first as a sign of this very thing: so all the saints who lived upon the earth previous to the birth of our Lord Jesus Christ, although they were born antecedently, were nevertheless united under the Head with that universal body of which He is the Head.

Chapter 20. —Of Israel's Bondage in Egypt, Their Deliverance, and Their Passage Through the Red Sea.

34. "That people, then, having been brought down into Egypt, were in bondage to the harshest of kings; and, taught by the most oppressive labors, they sought their deliverer in God; and there was sent to them one belonging to the people themselves, Moses, the holy servant of God, who, in the might of God, terrified the impious nation of the Egyptians in those days by great miracles, and led forth the people of God out of that land through the Red Sea, where the water parted and opened up a way for them as they crossed it, whereas, when the Egyptians pressed on in pursuit, the waves returned to their channel and overwhelmed them, so that they perished. Thus, then, just as the earth through the agency of the flood was cleansed by the waters from the wickedness of the sinners, who in those times were destroyed in their inundation, while the righteous escaped by means of the wood; so the people of God, when they went forth from Egypt, found a way through the waters by which their enemies were devoured. Nor was the sacrament of the wood wanting there. For Moses smote with his rod, in order that that miracle might be effected. Both these are signs of holy baptism, by which the faithful

pass into the new life, while their sins are done away with like enemies, and perish. But more clearly was the passion of Christ prefigured in the case of that people, when they were commanded to slay and eat the lamb, and to mark their door-posts with its blood, and to celebrate this rite every year, and to designate it the Lord's Passover. For surely prophecy speaks with the utmost plainness of the Lord Jesus Christ, when it says that "He was led as a lamb to the slaughter." And with the sign of His passion and cross, thou art this day to be marked on thy forehead, as on the door-post, and all Christians are marked with the same.

35. "Thereafter this people was conducted through the wilderness for forty years. They also received the law written by the finger of God, under which name the Holy Spirit is signified, as it is declared with the utmost plainness in the Gospel. For God is not defined by the form of a body, neither are members and fingers to be thought of as existent in Him in the way in which we see them in ourselves. But, inasmuch as it is through the Holy Spirit that God's gifts are divided to His saints, in order that, although they vary in their capacities, they may nevertheless not lapse from the concord of charity, and inasmuch as it is especially in the fingers that there appears a certain kind of division, while nevertheless there is no separation from unity, this may be the explanation of the phrase. But whether this may be the case, or whatever other reason may be assigned for the Holy Spirit being called the finger of God, we ought not at any rate to think of the form of a human body when we hear this expression used. The people in question, then, received the law written by the finger of God, and that in good sooth on tables of stone, to signify the hardness of their heart in that they were not to fulfill the law. For, as they eagerly sought from the Lord gifts meant for the uses of the body, they were held by carnal fear rather than by spiritual charity. But nothing fulfills the law save charity. Consequently, they were burdened with many visible sacraments, to the intent that they should feel the pressure of the yoke of bondage in the observances of meats, and in the sacrifices of animals, and in other rites innumerable; which things, at the same time,

were signs of spiritual matters relating to the Lord Jesus Christ and to the Church; which, furthermore, at that time were both understood by a few holy men to the effect of yielding the fruit of salvation, and observed by them in accordance with the fitness of the time, while by the multitude of carnal men they were observed only and not understood.

36. "In this manner, then, through many varied signs of things to come, which it would be tedious to enumerate in complete detail, and which we now see in their fulfillment in the Church, that people were brought to the land of promise, in which they were to reign in a temporal and carnal way in accordance with their own longings: which earthly kingdom, nevertheless, sustained the image of a spiritual kingdom. There Jerusalem was founded, that most celebrated city of God, which, while in bondage, served as a sign of the free city, which is called the heavenly Jerusalem which latter term is a Hebrew word, and signifies by interpretation the 'vision of peace.' The citizens thereof are all sanctified men, who have been, who are, and who are yet to be; and all sanctified spirits, even as many as are obedient to God with pious devotion in the exalted regions of heaven, and imitate not the impious pride of the devil and his angels. The King of this city is the Lord Jesus Christ, the Word of God, by whom the highest angels are governed, and at the same time the Word that took unto Himself human nature, in order that by Him men also might be governed, who, in His fellowship, shall reign all together in eternal peace. In the service of prefiguring this King in that earthly kingdom of the people of Israel, King David stood forth pre-eminent, of whose seed according to the flesh that truest King was to come, to wit, our Lord Jesus Christ, 'who is over all, God blessed forever.' In that land of promise many things were done, which held good as figures of the Christ who was to come, and of the Church, with which you will have it in your power to acquaint yourself by degrees in the Holy Books.

Chapter 21. —Of the Babylonish Captivity, and the Things Signified Thereby.

37. "Howbeit, after the lapse of some generations, another type was presented, which bears very emphatically on the matter in hand. For that city was brought into captivity, and a large section of the people were carried off into Babylonia. Now, as Jerusalem signifies the city and fellowship of the saints, so Babylonia signifies the city and fellowship of the wicked, seeing that by interpretation it denotes confusion. On the subject of these two cities, which have been running their courses, mingling the one with the other, through all the changes of time from the beginning of the human race, and which shall so move on together until the end of the world, when they are destined to be separated at the last judgment, we have spoken already a little ago. That captivity, then, of the city of Jerusalem, and the people thus carried into Babylonia in bondage, were ordained so to proceed by the Lord, by the voice of Jeremiah, a prophet of that time. And there appeared kings of Babylon, under whom they were in slavery, who on occasion of the captivity of this people were so wrought upon by certain miracles that they came to know the one true God who founded universal creation, and worshipped Him, and commanded that He should be worshipped. Moreover, the people were ordered both to pray for those by whom they were detained in captivity, and in their peace to hope for peace, to the effect that they should beget children, and build houses, and plant gardens and vineyards. But at the end of seventy years, release from their captivity was promised to them. All this, furthermore, signified in a figure that the Church of Christ in all His saints, who are citizens of the heavenly Jerusalem, would have to do service under the kings of this world. For the doctrine of the apostles speaks also in this wise, that 'every soul should be subject to the higher powers,' and that there 'should be rendered all things to all men, tribute to whom tribute (is due), custom to whom custom,' and all

other things in like manner which, without detriment to the worship of our God, we render to the rulers in the constitution of human society: for the Lord Himself also, in order to set before us an example of this sound doctrine, did not deem it unworthy of Him to pay tribute on account of that human individuality wherewith He was invested. Again, Christian servants and good believers are also commanded to serve their temporal masters in equanimity and faithfulness; whom they will hereafter judge, if even on to the end they find them wicked, or with whom they will hereafter reign in equality, if they too shall have been converted to the true God. Still all are enjoined to be subject to the powers that are of man and of earth, even until, at the end of the predetermined time which the seventy years signify, the Church shall be delivered from the confusion of this world, like as Jerusalem was to be set free from the captivity in Babylonia. By occasion of that captivity, however, the kings of earth too have themselves been led to forsake the idols on account of which they were wanting to persecute the Christians, and have come to know, and now worship, the one true God and Christ the Lord; and it is on their behalf that the Apostle Paul enjoins prayer to be made, even although they should persecute the Church. For he speaks in these terms: 'I entreat, therefore, that first of all supplications, adorations, intercessions, and givings of thanks be made for kings, for all men, and all that are in authority, that we may lead a quiet and peaceable life, with all godliness and charity.' Accordingly, peace has been given to the Church by these same persons, although it be but of a temporal sort, —a temporal quiet for the work of building houses after a spiritual fashion, and planting gardens and vineyards. For witness your own case, too, —at this very time we are engaged, by means of this discourse, in building you up and planting you. And the like process is going on throughout the whole circle of lands, in virtue of the peace allowed by Christian kings, even as the same apostle thus expresses himself: 'Ye are God's husbandry; ye are God's building.'

38. "And, indeed, after the lapse of the seventy years

of which Jeremiah had mystically prophesied, to the intent of prefiguring the end of times, with a view still to the perfecting of that same figure, no settled peace and liberty were conceded again to the Jews. Thus, it was that they were conquered subsequently by the Romans and made tributary. From that period, in truth, at which they received the land of promise and began to have kings, in order to preclude the supposition that the promise of the Christ who was to be their Liberator had met its complete fulfillment in the person of any one of their kings, Christ was prophesied of with greater clearness in a number of prophecies; not only by David himself in the book of Psalms, but also by the rest of the great and holy prophets, even on to the time of their conveyance into captivity in Babylonia; and in that same captivity there were also prophets whose mission was to prophesy of the coming of the Lord Jesus Christ as the Liberator of all. And after the restoration of the temple, when the seventy years had passed, the Jews sustained grievous oppressions and sufferings at the hands of the kings of the Gentiles, fitted to make them understand that the Liberator was not yet come, whom they failed to apprehend as one who was to effect for them a spiritual deliverance, and whom they fondly longed for on account of a carnal liberation.

Chapter 22. —Of the Six Ages of the World.

39. "Five ages of the world, accordingly, having been now completed (there has entered the sixth). Of these ages, the first is from the beginning of the human race, that is, from Adam, who was the first man that was made, down to Noah, who constructed the ark at the time of the flood. Then the second extends from that period on to Abraham, who was called the father indeed of all nations which should follow the example of his faith, but who at the same time in the way of natural descent from his own flesh was the father of the destined people of the Jews; which people, previous to the entrance of the Gentiles into the Christian faith, was the one people among all the nations of all lands that

worshipped the one true God: from which people also Christ the Savior was decreed to come according to the flesh. For these turning-points of those two ages occupy an eminent place in the ancient books. On the other hand, those of the other three ages are also declared in the Gospel, where the descent of the Lord Jesus Christ according to the flesh is likewise mentioned. For the third age extends from Abraham on to David the king; the fourth from David on to that captivity whereby the people of God passed over into Babylonia; and the fifth from that transmigration down to the advent of our Lord Jesus Christ. With His coming the sixth age has entered on its process; so that now the spiritual grace, which in previous times was known to a few patriarchs and prophets, may be made manifest to all nations; to the intent that no man should worship God but freely, fondly desiring of Him not the visible rewards of His services and the happiness of this present life, but that eternal life alone in which he is to enjoy God Himself: in order that in this sixth age the mind of man may be renewed after the image of God, even as on the sixth day man was made after the image of God. For then, too, is the law fulfilled, when all that it has commanded is done, not in the strong desire for things temporal, but in the love of Him who has given the commandment. Who is there, moreover, who should not be earnestly disposed to give the return of love to a God of supreme righteousness and also of supreme mercy, who has first loved men of the greatest unrighteousness and the loftiest pride, and that, too, so deeply as to have sent in their behalf His only Son, by whom He made all things, and who being made man, not by any change of Himself, but by the assumption of human nature, was designed thus to become capable not only of living with them, but also of dying at once for them and by their hands?

40. "Thus, then, showing forth the New Testament of our everlasting inheritance, wherein man was to be renewed by the grace of God and lead a new life, that is, a spiritual life; and with the view of exhibiting the first one as an old dispensation, wherein a carnal people acting out the old man (with the exception of a few patriarchs and

prophets, who had understanding, and some hidden saints), and leading a carnal life, desiderated carnal rewards at the hands of the Lord God, and received in that fashion but the figures of spiritual blessings;—with this intent, I say, the Lord Christ, when made man, despised all earthly good things, in order that He might show us how these things ought to be despised; and He endured all earthly ills which He was inculcating as things needful to be endured; so that neither might our happiness be sought for in the former class, nor our unhappiness be apprehended in the latter. For being born of a mother who, although she conceived without being touched by man and always remained thus untouched, in virginity conceiving, in virginity bringing forth, in virginity dying, had nevertheless been espoused to a handicraftsman, He extinguished all the inflated pride of carnal nobility. Moreover, being born in the city of Bethlehem, which among all the cities of Judea was so insignificant that even in our own day it is designated a village, He willed not that anyone should glory in the exalted position of any city of earth. He, too, whose are all things and by whom all things were created, was made poor, in order that no one, while believing in Him, might venture to boast himself in earthly riches. He refused to be made by men a king, because He displayed the pathway of humility to those unhappy ones whom pride had separated from Him; and yet universal creation attests the fact of His everlasting kingdom. An hungered was He who feeds all men; athirst was He by whom is created whatsoever is drunk, and who in a spiritual manner is the bread of the hungry and the fountain of the thirsty; in journeying on earth, wearied was He who has made Himself the way for us into heaven; as like one dumb and deaf in the presence of His revilers was He by whom the dumb spoke and the deaf heard; bound was He who freed us from the bonds of infirmities; scourged was He who expelled from the bodies of man the scourges of all distresses; crucified was He who put an end to our crucial pains; dead did He become who raised the dead. But He also rose again, no more to die, so that no one should from Him learn so to contemn death as if he were never to live again.

Chapter 23. —Of the Mission of the Holy Ghost Fifty Days After Christ's Resurrection.

41. "Thereafter, having confirmed the disciples, and having sojourned with them forty days, He ascended up into heaven, as these same persons were beholding Him. And on the completion of fifty days from His resurrection He sent to them the Holy Spirit (for so He had promised), by whose agency they were to have love shed abroad in their hearts, to the end that they might be able to fulfill the law, not only without the sense of its being burdensome, but even with a joyful mind. This law was given to the Jews in the ten commandments, which they call the Decalogue. And these commandments, again, are reduced to two, namely that we should love God with all our heart, with all our soul, with all our mind; and that we should love our neighbor as ourselves. For that on these two precepts hang all the law and the prophets, the Lord Himself has at once declared in the Gospel and shown in His own example. For thus it was likewise in the instance of the people of Israel, that from the day on which they first celebrated the Passover in a form, slaying and eating the sheep, with whose blood their door-posts were marked for the securing of their safety, —from this day, I repeat, the fiftieth day in succession was completed, and then they received the law written by the finger of God, under which phrase we have already stated that the Holy Spirit is signified. And in the same manner, after the passion and resurrection of the Lord, who is the true Passover, the Holy Ghost was sent personally to the disciples on the fiftieth day: not now, however, by tables of stone significant of the hardness of their hearts; but, when they were gathered together in one place at Jerusalem itself, suddenly there came a sound from heaven, as if a violent blast were being borne onwards, and there appeared to them tongues cloven like fire, and they began to speak with tongues, in such a manner that all those who had come to them recognized each his own language (for in that city the

Jews were in the habit of assembling from every country wheresoever they had been scattered abroad, and had learned the diverse tongues of diverse nations); and thereafter, preaching Christ with all boldness, they wrought many signs in His name,—so much so, that as Peter was passing by, his shadow touched a certain dead person, and the man rose in life again.

42. "But when the Jews perceived so great signs to be wrought in the name of Him, whom, partly through ill-will and partly in ignorance, they crucified, some of them were provoked to persecute the apostles, who were His preachers; while others, on the contrary, marveling the more at this very circumstance, that so great miracles were being performed in the name of Him whom they had derided as one overborne and conquered by themselves, repented, and were converted, so that thousands of Jews believed on Him. For these parties were not bent now on craving at the hand of God temporal benefits and an earthly kingdom, neither did they look any more for Christ, the promised king, in a carnal spirit; but they continued in immortal fashion to apprehend and love Him, who in mortal fashion endured on their behalf at their own hands sufferings so heavy, and imparted to them the gift of forgiveness for all their sins, even down to the iniquity of His own blood, and by the example of His own resurrection unfolded immortality as the object which they should hope for and long for at His hands. Accordingly, now mortifying the earthly cravings of the old man, and inflamed with the new experience of the spiritual life, as the Lord had enjoined in the Gospel, they sold all that they had, and laid the price of their possessions at the feet of the apostles, in order that these might distribute to every man according as each had need; and living in Christian love harmoniously with each other, they did not affirm anything to be their own, but they had all things in common, and were one in soul and heart toward God. Afterwards these same persons also themselves suffered persecution in their flesh at the hands of the Jews, their carnal fellow-countrymen, and were dispersed abroad, to the end that, in consequence of their dispersion, Christ

should be preached more extensively, and that they themselves at the same time should be followers of the patience of their Lord. For He who in meekness had endured them, enjoined them in meekness to endure for His sake.

43. "Among those same persecutors of the saints the Apostle Paul had once also ranked; and he raged with eminent violence against the Christians. But, subsequently, he became a believer and an apostle, and was sent to preach the gospel to the Gentiles, suffering (in that ministry) things more grievous on behalf of the name of Christ than were those which he had done against the name of Christ. Moreover, in establishing churches throughout all the nations where he was sowing the seed of the gospel, he was wanting to give earnest injunction that, as these converts (coming as they did from the worship of idols and without experience in the worship of the one God) could not readily serve God in the way of selling and distributing their possessions, they should make offerings for the poor brethren among the saints who were in the churches of Judea which had believed in Christ. In this manner, the doctrine of the apostle constituted some to be, as it were, soldiers, and others to be, as it were, provincial tributaries, while it set Christ in the center of them like the corner-stone (in accordance with what had been announced before time by the prophet), in whom both parties, like walls advancing from different sides, that is to say, from Jews and from Gentiles, might be joined together in the affection of kinship. But at a later period heavier and more frequent persecutions arose from the unbelieving Gentiles against the Church of Christ, and day by day was fulfilled that prophetic word which the Lord spoke when He said, 'Behold, I send you as sheep in the midst of wolves.'

Chapter 24. —Of the Church in Its Likeness to a Vine Sprouting and Suffering Pruning.

44. "But that vine, which was spreading forth its fruitful shoots throughout the circle of lands, according as

had been prophesied about it, and as had been foretold by the Lord Himself, sprouted all the more luxuriantly in proportion as it was watered with richer streams of the blood of martyrs. And as these died in behalf of the truth of the faith in countless numbers throughout all lands, even the persecuting kingdoms themselves desisted, and were converted to the knowledge and worship of Christ, with the neck of their pride broken. Moreover, it behooved that this same vine should be pruned in accordance with the Lord's repeated predictions, and that the unfruitful twigs should be cut out of it, by which heresies and schisms were occasioned in various localities, under the name of Christ, on the part of men who sought not His glory but their own; whose oppositions, however, also served more and more to discipline the Church, and to test and illustrate both its doctrine and its patience.

45. "All these things, then, we now perceive to be realized precisely as we read of them in predictions uttered so long before the event. And as the first Christians, inasmuch as they did not see these things literally made good in their own day, were moved by miracles to believe them; so as regards ourselves, inasmuch as all these things have now been brought to pass exactly as we read of them in those books which were written a long time previous to the fulfillment of the things in question, wherein they were all announced as matters yet future, even as they are now seen to be actually present, we are built up unto faith, so that, enduring and persevering in the Lord, we believe without any hesitation in the destined accomplishment even of those things which still remain to be realized. For, indeed, in the same Scriptures, tribulations yet to come are still read of, as well as the final day of judgment itself, when all the citizens of these two states shall receive their bodies again, and rise and give account of their life before the judgment-seat of Christ. For He will come in the glory of His power, who of old condescended to come in the lowliness of humanity; and He will separate all the godly from the ungodly, —not only from those who have utterly refused to believe in Him at all, but also from those who have believed in Him to no purpose

and without fruit. To the one class He will give an eternal kingdom together with Himself, while to the other He will award eternal punishment together with the devil. But as no joy yielded by things temporal can be found in any measure comparable to the joy of life eternal which the saints are destined to attain, so no torment of temporal punishments can be compared to the everlasting torments of the unrighteous.

Chapter 25. —Of Constancy in the Faith of the Resurrection.

46. "Therefore, brother, confirm yourself in the name and help of Him in whom you believe, so as to withstand the tongues of those who mock at our faith, in whose case the devil speaks seductive words, bent above all on making a mockery of the faith in a resurrection. But, judging from your own history, believe that, seeing you have been, you will also be hereafter, even as you perceive yourself now to be, although previously you were not. For where was this great structure of your body, and where this formation and compacted connection of members a few years ago, before you were born, or even before you were conceived in your mother's womb? Where, I repeat, was then this structure and this stature of your body? Did it not come forth to light from the hidden secrets of this creation, under the invisible formative operations of the Lord God, and did it not rise to its present magnitude and fashion by those fixed measures of increase which come with the successive periods of life? Is it then in any way a difficult thing for God, who also in a moment brings together out of secrecy the masses of the clouds and veils the heavens in an instant of time, to make this quantity of your body again what it was, seeing that He was able to make it what formerly it was not? Consequently, believe with a manful and unshaken spirit that all those things which seem to be withdrawn from the eyes of men as if to perish, are safe and exempt from loss in relation to the omnipotence of God, who will restore them, without any delay or difficulty, when

He is so minded,—those of them at least, I should say, that are judged by His justice to merit restoration; in order that men may give account of their deeds in their very bodies in which they have done them; and that in these they may be deemed worthy to receive either the exchange of heavenly incorruption in accordance with the deserts of their piety, or the corruptible condition of body in accordance with the deserts of their wickedness,—and that, too, not a condition such as may be done away with by death, but such as shall furnish material for everlasting pains.

47. "Flee, therefore, by steadfast faith and good manners, —flee, brother, those torments in which neither the torturers fail, nor do the tortured die; to whom it is death without end, to be unable to die in their pains. And be kindled with love and longing for the everlasting life of the saints, in which neither will action be toilsome nor will rest be indolent; in which the praise of God will be without irksomeness and without defect; wherein there will be no weariness in the mind, no exhaustion in the body; wherein, too, there shall be no want, whether on your own part, so that you should crave for relief, or on your neighbor's part, so that you should be in haste to carry relief to him. God will be the whole enjoyment and satisfaction of that holy city, which lives in Him and of Him, in wisdom and beatitude. For as we hope and look for what has been promised by Him, we shall be made equal to the angels of God, and together with them we shall enjoy that Trinity now by sight, wherein at present we walk by faith. For we believe that which we see not, in order that through these very deserts of faith we may be counted worthy also to see that which we believe, and to abide in it; to the intent that these mysteries of the equality of the Father, the Son, and the Holy Spirit, and the unity of this same Trinity, and the manner in which these three subsistences are one God, need no more be uttered by us in words of faith and sounding syllables, but may be drunk in in purest and most burning contemplation in that silence.

48. "These things hold fixed in your heart, and call upon the God in whom you believe, to defend you against

the temptations of the devil; and be careful, lest that adversary come stealthily upon you from a strange quarter, who, as a most malevolent solace for his own damnation, seeks others whose companionship he may obtain in that damnation. For he is bold enough not only to tempt Christian people through the instrumentality of those who hate the Christian name, or are pained to see the world taken possession of by that name, and still fondly desire to do service to idols and to the curious rites of evil spirits, but at times he also attempts the same through the agency of such men as we have mentioned a little ago, to wit, persons severed from the unity of the Church, like the twigs which are lopped off when the vine is pruned, who are called heretics or schismatics. Howbeit sometimes also he makes the same effort by means of the Jews, seeking to tempt and seduce believers by their instrumentality. Nevertheless, what ought above all things to be guarded against is, that no individual may suffer himself to be tempted and deceived by men who are within the Catholic Church itself, and who are borne by it like the chaff that is sustained against the time of its winnowing. For in being patient toward such persons, God has this end in view, namely, to exercise and confirm the faith and prudence of His elect by means of the perverseness of these others while at the same time He also takes account of the fact that many of their number make an advance, and are converted to the doing of the good pleasure of God with a great impetus, when led to take pity upon their own souls. For not all treasure up for themselves, through the patience of God, wrath in the day of the wrath of His just judgment; but many are brought by the same patience of the Almighty to the most wholesome pain of repentance. And until that is effected, they are made the means of exercising not only the forbearance, but also the compassion of those who are already holding by the right way. Accordingly, you will have to witness many drunkards, covetous men, deceivers gamesters, adulterers, fornicators, men who bind upon their persons sacrilegious charms and others given up to sorcerers and astrologers, and diviners practiced in all kinds of impious arts. You will also have to observe how those very crowds which fill the theatres on the festal days of the pagans also fill the churches on the festal days of the Christians. And when you see these things you will be tempted to imitate them. Nay, why should I use the expression, you will see, about what you assuredly are acquainted with even already? For you are not ignorant of the fact that many who are called Christians engage in all these evil things which I have briefly mentioned. Neither are you ignorant that at times, perchance, men whom you know to bear the name of Christians are guilty of even more grievous offenses than these. But if you have come with the notion that you may do such things as in a secured position, you are greatly in error; neither will the name of Christ be of any avail to you when He begins to judge in utmost strictness, who also of old condescended in utmost mercy to come to man's relief. For He Himself has foretold these things, and speaks to this effect in the Gospel: 'Not everyone that saith unto me, Lord, Lord, shall enter into the kingdom of heaven; but he that doeth the will of my Father. Many shall say unto me in that day, Lord, Lord, in thy name we have eaten and drunken.' For all, therefore, who persevere in such works the end is damnation. Consequently, when you see many not only doing these things but also defending and recommending them, keep yourself firmly by the law of God, and follow not its willful transgressors. For it is not according to their mind, but according to His truth that you will be judged.

49. "Associate with the good, whom you perceive to be at one with you in loving your King. For there are many such for you to discover, if you also begin to cultivate that character yourself. For if in the public spectacles you wished to be in congenial company, and to attach yourself closely to men who are united with you in a liking for some charioteer, or some hunter, or some player or other, how much more ought you to find pleasure in associating with those who are at one with you in loving that God, with regard to whom no one that loves Him shall ever have cause for the blush of shame, inasmuch as not only is He Himself incapable of being overcome, but He will also render those

unconquerable who are affectionately disposed toward Him. At the same time, not even on those same good men, who either anticipate you or accompany you on the way to God, ought you to set your hope, seeing that no more ought you to place it on yourself, however great may be the progress you have made, but on Him who justifies both them and you, and thus makes you what you are. For you are secure in God, because He changes not; but in man no one prudently counts himself secure. But if we ought to love those who are not righteous as yet, with the view that they may be so, how much more warmly ought those to be loved who already are righteous? At the same time, it is one thing to love man, and another thing to set one's hope in man; and the difference is so great, that God enjoins the one and forbids the other. Moreover, if you have to sustain either any insults or any sufferings in the cause of the name of Christ, and neither fall away from the faith nor decline from the good way, you are certain to receive the greater reward; whereas those who give way to the devil in such circumstances, lose even the less reward. But be humble toward God, in order that He may not permit you to be tempted beyond your strength."

Chapter 26. —Of the Formal Admission of the Catechumen, and of the Signs Therein Made Use of.

50. At the conclusion of this address the person is to be asked whether he believes these things and earnestly desires to observe them. And on his replying to that effect then certainly he is to be solemnly signed and dealt with in accordance with the custom of the Church. On the subject of the sacrament, indeed, which he receives, it is first to be well impressed upon his notice that the signs of divine things are, it is true, things visible, but that the invisible things themselves are also honored in them, and that that species, which is then sanctified by the blessing, is therefore not to be regarded merely in the way in which it is regarded in any common use. And thereafter he ought to be told what is also signified by the form of words to which he has listened, and what in him is seasoned by that (spiritual grace) of which

this material substance presents the emblem. Next we should take occasion by that ceremony to admonish him that, if he hears anything even in the Scriptures which may carry a carnal sound, he should, even although he fails to understand it, nevertheless believe that something spiritual is signified thereby, which bears upon holiness of character and the future life. Moreover, in this way he learns briefly that, whatever he may hear in the canonical books of such a kind as to make him unable to refer it to the love of eternity, and of truth, and of sanctity, and to the love of our neighbor, he should believe that to have been spoken or done with a figurative significance; and that, consequently, he should endeavor to understand it in such a manner as to refer it to that twofold (duty of) love. He should be further admonished, however, not to take the term neighboring a carnal sense, but to understand under it everyone who may ever be with him in that holy city, whether there already or not yet apparent. And (he should finally be counselled) not to despair of the amendment of any man whom he perceives to be living under the patience of God for no other reason, as the apostle says, than that he may be brought to repentance.

51. If this discourse, in which I have supposed myself to have been teaching some uninstructed person in my presence, appears to you to be too long, you are at liberty to expound these matters with greater brevity. I do not think, however, that it ought to be longer than this. At the same time, much depends on what the case itself, as it goes on, may render advisable, and what the audience actually present shows itself not only to bear, but also to desire. When, however, rapid dispatch is required, notice with what facility the whole matter admits of being explained. Suppose once more that someone comes before us who desires to be a Christian; and accordingly, suppose further that he has been interrogated, and that he has returned the answer which we have taken the former catechumen to have given; for, even should he decline to make this reply, it must at least be said that he ought to have given it; —then all that remains to be said to him should be put together in the following manner: —

52. Of a truth, brother, that is great and true blessedness which is promised to the saints in a future world. All visible things, on the other hand, pass away, and all the pomp, and pleasure, and solicitude1504of this world will perish, and (even now) they drag those who love them along with them onward to destruction. The merciful God, willing to deliver men from this destruction, that is to say, from everlasting pains, if they should not prove enemies to themselves, and if they should not withstand the mercy of their Creator, sent His only begotten Son, that is to say, His Word, equal with Himself, by whom He made all things. And He, while abiding indeed in His divinity, and neither receding from the Father nor being changed in anything, did at the same time, by taking on Himself human nature, and appearing to men in mortal flesh, come unto men; in order that, just as death entered among the human race by one man, to wit, the first that was made, that is to say, Adam, because he consented unto his wife when she was seduced by the devil to the effect that they (both) transgressed the commandment of God; even so by one man, Jesus Christ, who is also God, the Son of God, all those who believe in Him might have all their past sins done away with, and enter into eternal life.

Chapter 27. —Of the Prophecies of the Old Testament in Their Visible Fulfillment in the Church.

53. "For all those things, which at present you witness in the Church of God, and which you see to be taking place under the name of Christ throughout the whole world, were predicted long ages ago. And even as we read of them, so also we now see them. And by means of these things we are built up unto faith. Once of old there occurred a flood over the whole earth, the object of which was that sinners might be destroyed. And, nevertheless, those who escaped in the ark exhibited a sacramental sign of the Church that was to be, which at present is floating on the waves of the world, and is delivered from submersion by the wood of the cross of Christ. It was predicted to Abraham, a

faithful servant of God, a single man, that of Him it was determined that a people should be born who should worship one God in the midst of all other nations which worshipped idols; and all things which were prophesied of as destined to happen to that people have come to pass exactly as they were foretold. Among that people Christ, the King of all saints and their God, was also prophesied of as destined to come of the seed of that same Abraham according to the flesh, which (flesh) He took unto Himself, in order that all those also who became followers of His faith might be sons of Abraham; and thus it has come to pass: Christ was born of the Virgin Mary, who belonged to that race. It was foretold by the prophets that He would suffer on the cross at the hands of that same people of the Jews, of whose lineage, according to the flesh, He came; and thus it has come to pass. It was foretold that He would rise again: He has risen again; and, in accordance with these same predictions of the prophets, He has ascended into heaven and has sent the Holy Spirit to His disciples. It was foretold not only by the prophets, but also by the Lord Jesus Christ Himself, that His Church would exist throughout the whole world, extended by the martyrdoms and sufferings of the saints; and this was foretold at a time when as yet His name was at once undeclared to the Gentiles, and made a subject of derision where it was known; and, nevertheless, in the power of His miracles, whether those which He wrought by His own hand or those which he effected by means of His servants, as these things are being reported and believed, we already see the fulfillment of that which was predicted, and behold the very kings of the earth, who formerly were wont to persecute the Christians, even now brought into subjection to the name of Christ. It was also foretold that schisms and heresies would arise from His Church, and that under His name they would seek their own glory instead of Christ's, in such places as they might be able to command; and these predictions have been realized.

54. "Will those things, then, which yet remain fail to come to pass? It is manifest that, just as the former class of things which were foretold have come to pass, so will these

latter also come to pass. I refer to all the tribulations of the righteous, which yet wait for fulfillment, and to the day of judgment, which will separate all the wicked from the righteous in the resurrection of the dead; —and not only will it thus separate those wicked men who are outside the Church, but also it will set apart for the fire, which is due to such, the chaff of the Church itself, which must be borne with in utmost patience on to the last winnowing. Moreover, they who deride the (doctrine of a) resurrection, because they think that this flesh, inasmuch as it becomes corrupt, cannot rise again, will certainly rise in the same unto punishment, and God will make it plain to such, that He who was able to form these bodies when as yet they were not, is able in a moment to restore them as they were. But all the faithful who are destined to reign with Christ shall rise with the same body in such wise that they may also be counted worthy to be changed into angelic incorruption; so that they may be made equal unto the angels of God, even as the Lord Himself has promised; and that they may praise Him without any failure and without any weariness, ever living in Him and of Him, with such joy and blessedness as can be neither expressed nor conceived by man.

55. "Believe these things, therefore, and be on your guard against temptations (for the devil seeks for others who may be brought to perish along with himself); so that not only may that adversary fail to seduce you by the help of those who are without the Church, whether they be pagans, or Jews, or heretics; but you yourself also may decline to follow the example of those within the Catholic Church itself whom you see leading an evil life, either indulging in excess in the pleasures of the belly and the throat, or unchaste, or given up to the vain and unlawful observances of curious superstitions, whether they be addicted to (the inanities of) public spectacles, or charms, or divinations of devils, or be living in the pomp and inflated arrogance of covetousness and pride, or be pursuing any sort of life which the law condemns and punishes. But rather connect yourself with the good, whom you will easily find out, if you yourself were once become of that character; so that you may unite with

each other in worshipping and loving God for His own sake; for He himself will be our complete reward to the intent that we may enjoy His goodness and beauty in that life. He is to be loved, however, not in the way in which any object that is seen with the eyes is loved, but as wisdom is loved, and truth, and holiness, and righteousness, and charity, and whatever else may be mentioned as of kindred nature; and further, with a love conformable to these things not as they are in men, but as they are in the very fountain of incorruptible and unchangeable wisdom. Whomsoever, therefore, you may observe to be loving these things, attach yourself to them, so that through Christ, who became man in order that He might be the Mediator between God and men, you may be reconciled to God.

But as regards the perverse, even if they find their way within the walls of the Church, think not that they will find their way into the kingdom of heaven; for in their own time they will be set apart, if they have not altered to the better. Consequently, follow the example of good men, bear with the wicked, love all; forasmuch as you know not what he will be to-morrow who to-day is evil. Howbeit, love not the unrighteousness of such; but love the persons themselves with the express intent that they may apprehend righteousness; for not only is the love of God enjoined upon us, but also the love of our neighbor, on which two commandments hang all the law and the prophets. And this is fulfilled by no one save the man who has received the (other) gift, the Holy Spirit, who is indeed equal with the Father and with the Son; for this same Trinity is God; and on this God every hope ought to be placed. On man our hope ought not to be placed, of whatsoever character he may be. For He, by whom we are justified, is one thing; and they, together with whom we are justified, are another. Moreover, it is not only by lusts that the devil tempts, but also by the terrors of insults, and pains, and death itself. But whatever a man shall have suffered on behalf of the name of Christ, and for the sake of the hope of eternal life, and shall have endured in constancy, (in accordance therewith) the greater reward shall be given him; whereas, if he shall give way to the devil, he shall be damned along with him. But works of mercy, conjoined with pious humility, meet with this acknowledgment from God, to wit, that He will not suffer His servants to be tempted more than they are able to bear."

www.ingramcontent.com/pod-product-compliance
Lightning Source LLC
Chambersburg PA
CBHW052114070526
44584CB00017B/2485